Sumud

Gender, Culture, and Politics in the Middle East
miriam cooke, Simona Sharoni, and Suad Joseph, *Series Editors*

For a full list of titles in this series,
visit https://press.syr.edu/supressbook-series
/gender-culture-and-politics-in-the-middle-east/.

SUMUD

Birth, Oral History, and Persisting in Palestine

Livia Wick

Syracuse University Press

∞ The paper used in this publication meets the minimum requirements
of the American National Standard for Information Sciences—Permanence
of Paper for Printed Library Materials, ANSI Z39.48-1992.

For a listing of books published and distributed by Syracuse University Press,
visit https://press.syr.edu/.

ISBN: 978-0-8156-3779-0 (hardcover)
978-0-8156-3788-2 (paperback)
978-0-8156-5572-5 (e-book)

Library of Congress Cataloging-in-Publication Data
Names: Wick, Livia, author.
Title: Sumud : birth, oral history, and persisting in Palestine / Livia Wick.
Description: First edition. | Syracuse : Syracuse University Press, 2023. | Series: Gender, culture,
and politics in the Middle East | Includes bibliographical references and index.
Identifiers: LCCN 2022030211 (print) | LCCN 2022030212 (ebook) | ISBN 9780815637790 (hardback) |
ISBN 9780815637882 (paperback) | ISBN 9780815655725 (ebook)
Subjects: LCSH: Childbirth—Palestine. | Midwifery—Palestine. | Midwives—Palestine—Interviews. |
Women, Palestinian Arab—Health and hygiene—Israel. | Mutual health organizations—Palestine.
Classification: LCC RG963.P35 W53 2023 (print) | LCC RG963.P35 (ebook) |
DDC 362.19840095694—dc23/eng/20220913
LC record available at https://lccn.loc.gov/2022030211
LC ebook record available at https://lccn.loc.gov/2022030212

Manufactured in the United States of America

Contents

Acknowledgments

Without the generosity of many people, this book would not have been possible. For institutional support that freed me from other responsibilities, I want to thank the fellowships at the MIT program in the Anthropology and History of Science, Technology, and Society, the Dissertation Research Grant from the Middle East Awards Program in Population and the Social Sciences (MEA awards), the Palestinian American Research Center (PARC) Fellowship, the Wenner Gren Foundation Post-PhD Research Grant, and the American University of Beirut Periodic Paid Research Leave.

I thank my editor, Margaret Solic, at Syracuse University Press for helping cultivate this book and providing professional, kind, and thoughtful reflection. I thank the anonymous reviewers whose comments made the text deeper and more coherent. And I thank Malak Mattar for the picture of her beautiful painting on the cover.

I want to thank the people I met, interviewed, and worked with during my fieldwork in Palestine. They include many people. They were generous and courageous. Sometimes we met under difficult circumstances, under curfew or in between sieges. These conditions didn't deter from passionate discussions.

This book took a long time to write. It started as a dissertation project. My advisor, Michael M. J. Fischer will see his imprint on most pages of the book. He taught, mentored, supported, and followed the project through all its stages. His intellectual insights have become essential to the way I do anthropology.

Other scholars at MIT influenced the course of this book. Joseph Dumit's deep curiosity and acceptance of many intellectual traditions, fields of work, and ways of being in academia encouraged me to keep thinking. He constantly opened new paths of inquiry and for that I am grateful. Harriet Ritvo's attention to language and history pushed me through the grueling efforts of working on my writing. When I reread parts of the manuscript, I still remember her funny comments pushing me to continue writing. Aslihan Sanal was two years ahead of me in the doctoral program. From the first day, we became close friends. She mentored me and identified for me the importance of the gifts of being able to listen. She helped me read, interpret, and prepare class presentations. I visited her during her fieldwork in Istanbul in the summer of 2001 and read her writing. Her ethnography shifted the lens through which I was seeing my own work.

Colleagues and friends at MIT, and in the Boston area more generally, listened, commented, and provided support at different times. They include Orkideh Behrouzan, Sandy Brown, Candice Callison, Anita Chan, Omar Dewachi, Eleanor Doumato, Deborah Fitzgerald, Chantal Fujiwara Levi-Alvarez, Byron Good, Nate Greenslit, Hugh Gusterson, Shane Hamilton, Evelynn Hammonds, Clara Han, Meg Hiesinger, Yamila Hussein, Hyun Gyun Im, Helene Izidi, Erica James, David Kaiser, Wen Hua Kuo, Dave Lukso, Eden Miller Medina, Rob Meijers, Natasha Myers, Sarah Pinto, Anne Pollock, Rachel Prentice, Jenny Smith, Merrit Roe Smith, Susan Slyomovics, Kaushik Sunder Rajan, Bill Turkle, Pirooz Vakili, Susanne Wilkinson, Rosalind Williams, Anya Zilberstein, and finally Esra Ozkan, who became a close friend. Indeed, Esra's readings, presence, and support cultivated this project at crucial times. And in Providence, I thank my teachers and friends, Engin Akarli, Cagla Aykac, Lundy Braun, Eleanor Dumato, Martha Jokowsky, Amer Khayyat, Iris Kulasic, Armando Manalo, Zeina Mobassaleh, Dima Reda, and Danya Reda. In Paris, I thank Raphael Botiveau, Nadia El Issa Mondeguer, Henry Laurens, Olivier Pironet, and Irene, Maria, and Cristina Gurrado.

Friends and teachers in Palestine contributed to this book in their own way: Deema Arafah, Annie Flamant, Sahar Hassan, Donn Hutchinson, Nadia Abboushi, Rana Hutchinson, Ramzi Hutchinson, Anna Kennedy, Dima Khalidi, Rama Meri, Mollie Milesi, Claude and Youssef Abou Samra, Myriam and Karem Abou Samra, Musaddaq Al-Masri, Sylvia and Ezra Ovadia, and Adi, Zahra, Lara, Maya, and Sami al-Khalidi. Rita

Giacaman always took interest in my work and life. She provided support and inspiration at crucial moments of the work on this book. The late Adel Yahya had a formative influence on my brothers and me. His affection, courage, and energy touched us forever. With Natasha Khalidi, I share a friendship that began in first grade. We were neighbors and we jumped over the stone wall to visit each other. The years passed, our lives changed, and our friendship remained. It is a special thing to have someone in the world that you befriended when you were six and stayed friends with over decades and decades.

Since my PhD, I have worked at the American University of Beirut. There are many colleagues and students who in one way or another helped to write this book. The Department of Social and Behavioral Sciences (SBS), which became the Department of Sociology, Anthropology, and Media Studies (SOAM) has been my workplace. It brought people together and provided space for this book to come to light. SBS colleagues include: May Awaida, Maria Baramakian, Karma Bibi, Greg Burris, Josh Carney, Nabil Dajani, Arne Dietrich, Suzanne Enzerik, May Farah, Samar Ghanem, Sari Hanafi, Charles Harb, Sami Hermez, Anaheed Al-Hardan, Tima Al-Jamil, Leila Jbara, Samar Kanafani, Shahe Kazarian, Samir Khalaf, Munira Khayyat, Dina Kiwan, Maysa Kobrosly, Rima Majed, Muzna Al-Masri, Jad Melki, Marc Michael, Lamia Moghnie, Fuad Musallam, Sara Mourad, Nidal Najjar, Zeina Osman, Zina Sawwaf, the late Hussein Shahidi, and Nadya Slobodenyuk. Blake Atwood, the current chairperson, shared his knowledge of book publishing and I'm grateful for his help and advice. I worked with everyone in the department. But in the case of Sylvain Perdigon, Elizabeth Saleh, Kirsten Scheid, and Richard Saumarez Smith, we worked together intensely and constantly plotted and planned to strengthen the master's program in anthropology. I am grateful for the efforts, long discussions, disagreements, and friendship, and especially for sharing the work of accompanying our graduate students on their journey to write a thesis and become anthropologists. Richard and Kirsten laid the groundwork. Kirsten paved the way for the program to work independently with her persistence and devoted teaching. Richard complemented with his dedication to the yearly theory course and his knowledge of the history of the department. From 2017 to 2019, Sylvain was the only other anthropologist present in the department. I will not forget our trip to Tyre Beach with graduate students. We felt an intense connection with our students and our common journey. Elizabeth joined in 2018, carried the load of steering the program, and we became friends. I'm grateful for their friendship. The graduate students were vital in creating a space of connection and care. They were essential in my process of learning and thinking through this book: Asli Altinsik, Abdallah Ayyache, Marwa Bakabas, Nora Bakhsh, Susan Barclay, Ghada Dagher, Noor Daher, Carmen Feliz-Taveras, Ali Ghandour, Samar Ghanem, May Habib, Batoul Al-Hajj, Ruby Haji-Naif, Heghnar Heghiaian, Julianne Ivany, Rita Jarrous, Minou Hexpoor Machnouk, Rabih Hojeij, Ziad Kiblawi, Diana Khanafer, Araz Koyajan, Jennifer Levarge, Zhixi Liu, Shantanu Mehra, Luisa Meyer, Haya Mortada, Ghassan Moussawi, Natalie Nahas, Mariana Nakfour, Sarah Mallat, Hussein El-Moallem, Hibah Morcos, Rayane Al-Rammal, Lara Sabra, Hussein Shami, Soheila Shorbaji, Ramy Shukr, Mac Skelton, Annabel Turner, Karen Ravn Vestergaard, Jude Wafai, Natalie Wilkinson and Zeina Zayour.

Other colleagues and friends supported me and my family in my time working at AUB: the late Abdul Rahim Abu Hussein, Lila Abu-Lughod, Rima Afifi, Diana Allan, Lori Allen, Azza Barazi, Philippe Bourmaud, Nadia El-Cheikh, Ahmad Dallal, Jocelyn DeJong, Ilana Feldman, Moushira El-Geziri, Andre Gingrich, Farha Ghannam, Ibtissam Ghazzara, Ghassan Hage, Sherine Hamdy, Amina Hindawi, Zeina Halabi, Zeina Halabieh, Heghnar Heghiaian, Marcia Inhorn, Irene Maffi, Coralie Pison-Hindawi, Ruba Ismail, Afamia Kaddour, Tarif Khalidi, Abeer Khoury, Elisabeth Longuenesse, Zeina Mobassaleh, Cynthia Myntti, Patrick McGreevey, John Melloy, Iman Nuwayhid, Julie Peteet, Rima Rassi, Nadine Rizk, Yasmine Eid-Sabbagh, Walid Sadek, Aliya Saidi, Helen Samaha, Rosemary Sayigh, Seteni Shami, Petra Shenk, Asma Shihab, Selame Tsagaye, Belgin Tekce, Roham Yamout, Abbas El-Zein, Huda Zurayk, and the Khayyat family: Munira, Amer, Yasmine, Rola, Ghassan, Fadia, and the late Adnan.

My friendships in Beirut were essential to keeping me going through the process of writing this book. Mayssoun Sukkarieh has been a close family friend and collaborator for many years. Her visits, messages, and love sustain me on a daily basis. Certain friends were important parts of life and work in Beirut: Afamia Kaddour, Hibah Osman, Samer Frangie, Samer Farah, and Diana Zogheib. Beirut would be empty without Samer Farah's music and Diana's commentary on life. Since the beginning of the COVID-19 pandemic, my husband, Samer Jabbour, and I have gathered together each week with Sonja Mejcher-Atassi, Ali Atassi, Rabi'a Barazi and Fouad Mohamad Fouad. The children, Leen, Ghadi, Nour, Karim, Ramla, Naji, and Yamen sometimes join too. These gatherings sustain us as the city is sinking, transforming itself in rapid and terrifying ways.

Other groups also maintained my work and life in Beirut. I am grateful to the writing group with Muzna Al-Masri, Lamia Moghnieh, Samar Kanafani, Helena Nassif, Elizabeth Saleh, and Zina Sawwaf. We met at Mansion every two weeks in 2018. Their friendship, perspective, care, and critical eyes helped in rewriting parts of the manuscript. Muzna recommended I write in a way that would interest my daughter. Then in the fall of 2020, Muzna Al-Masri and Michelle Obeid co-organized the ethno-diaries project at the Arab Council for Social Sciences (ACSS). It brought together a group of thirteen writers in an attempt to record bits and pieces of city life. I thank Michelle, Muzna, and the other writers for the support and confidence it gave me in writing and sharing writing.

From Suad Joseph, I keep learning the art of bringing people together and building large research teams. I thank her for advice, support, and inspiration. I have learned from the other collaborators on the Gender and STEM education project: Linda Bisson, Clare Cannon, Dawn Gheng, Iman Osta, Mona Monfared, Danneal Jamison-McClung, Hanan Sabae, Dawn Summer, Ghada Karaki, and Martina Rieker.

The Reproductive Health Working Group in Arab Countries and Turkey (RHWG) has been a space of warmth, support, and intellectual stimulation. There are many at RHWG that have provided encouragement and ways of thinking in new ways. I name a few here and have surely forgotten some: Hanan Abdul Rahim, Niveen Abu Rmeileh, Can Açiksöz, Feyza Akinerdem, Hyam Bashour, Soha Bayoumi, Lenka Benova, Miral Breebart, Başak Can, Dalita Çetinoğlu, Jocelyn DeJong, Omar Dewachi, Niveen Hassanein, Tamar Kabakian, Faysal El Kak, Noha Gaballah, Farha Ghannam, Atf Gherissi, Rita Giacaman, Sherine Hamdy, Doaa Hammoudeh, Weeam Hammoudeh, Karima Khalil, Zeynep Korkman, Awad

Mataria, Cynthia Myntti, Hibah Osman, Hania Sholkamy, Nükhet Sir-
man, Belgin Tekçe, Ayşecan Terzioğlu, Yesim Yasin and Huda Zurayk.

I have been lucky to share a city of residence with my brother Ali
Wick. I cherish the times my children, husband, and I have had with Ali,
Dahlia Gubara, and their children, Amalia and Shams. They left Beirut. I
miss getting together and sharing life projects. I do not know if I will ever
live in the same city with natal kin again. Their thinking and writings
have shaped this book to the core. My brother Jamal Wick has been living
in Jordan and then the United Arab Emirates. Visits with him and Ale-
jandra Murillo, and now baby Emilio, are full of joy and care. While they
are in another line of work, their experiences and perspectives shape my
thinking. My mother-in-law, Lora Hilal, lives in Portland, Oregon, now.
She is a master storyteller. Sometimes I try to listen to how she weaves
things together to bring something of that to my writing. Our yearly visits
with her in Wausau, Wisconsin, have been a constant since my father-in-
law, Hanna Jabbour, died in 2016. The visits give sustenance and rhythm
to our family's life and remind us that we lost my father-in-law too early. I
also thank my sisters-in-law, Samar and Badia Jabbour, as well as Joud Jabbour and Riad Al-Harithy, for the fun times, hospitality, and love. I thank
my aunts Tina Sizemore, Wendy Reaves, and Sandy Ruggiero; as well as
their husbands, Mike Sizemore, John Daniel Reaves, Gary Ruggiero; and
their children, Christi and James Sizemore, Paul and Caroline Reaves, and
Jessie, Heather, Trevor, and Marika Ruggiero. I do not see them regularly
anymore. But they remain important referents in life. My late grandpar-
ents, Paul Wick and Christine Wick, and Marieluise Heacock, appear to
me through bouts of memory as I think of this book, life projects, and
death. My aunt Marion Heacock lives in Philadelphia, Pennsylvania. She
too visits yearly in Wausau, Wisconsin. I cherish our connection and
her openness, generosity, and curiosity. Finally, my parents, Laura Wick
and Roger Heacock. Their care has been vital. It is indescribable. Without them, this book would not have emerged with me. For my children,
Ramla, Naji, and Yamen, the book was always a part of their lives. Their
thinking, force, and creativity are an inspiration. What a joy it was the day
my teenage daughter and son read the first chapter. Finally, I thank my life
companion, Samer Jabbour. Our love nurtured the book and us.

Prologue

Return

I had forgotten my return to Ramallah to do fieldwork about birth in early June 2002, now twenty years ago. I rediscovered the story in my field notes as I started to write a beginning to this book. I arrived at the airport from the United States, went through airport security, took a collective taxi to Jerusalem, and crossed the Green Line from West Jerusalem to East Jerusalem. It was too late in the day to go to Ramallah. I slept in Jerusalem in a room my parents had rented years earlier in an Armenian convent. The next morning, I set out to go to the rented apartment in Ramallah. I got into a taxi, got off at the first checkpoint, and stood in line, with women in one line and men in the other. After waiting in line under the June sun for my turn, I showed my American passport to the soldier. "What do you do in Ramallah?" he asked. I said that I lived there. He let me through. I got into another collective taxi, to the next checkpoint. Three checkpoints later, I reached Ramallah. I arranged my things, bought groceries, and went to sleep. The next morning, I heard an Israeli military jeep announcing in microphones: *"Mamnou' al-tajawwol, mamnou' al-tajawwol ḥata ish'āran akhar,"* (Curfew, curfew until further notice). That sound I knew from my childhood. It was an order to get off the streets and into houses until the news broadcast announced new orders. So I stayed in the apartment for three days; I learned later that this would become a pattern that year.

Curfews are part of a set of Israeli policies in the Occupied Palestinian Territories known as the closure (*al-taskīr*). The closure restricts people's mobility through physical, military, legal and bureaucratic barriers, including checkpoints (*ḥājiz* or *maḥsūm*), the separation wall (*al-al-jiḍār*), restrictions on visas, military invasions (*ijtiyāḥ*), walled off streets, barbed wire, snipers (*qannāṣ*), a hierarchy of identification cards (*hawiyyāt*), three types of administrative/military areas—A, B, and C—and curfews (*man'al-tajawwul*). Closure separates cities, villages, and families from each other either temporarily or for the long term. In my dissertation (2006), I used the metaphor of "waiting zones" to discuss life under these spatial and temporal barriers. Under closure, people have the feeling that their world is shrinking and moving backwards or stagnating in time.

During curfews, people watch television. I spent my first three days watching Al-Jazeera. Founded in 1996, this news channel transformed the television landscape of the Middle East from state television stations (in Palestine it was Jordanian and Israeli state television broadcasts) to what Al-Jazeera called "the opinion, and the other opinion," a clause that became the channel's slogan and presentation method. It critiqued some dictatorships, such as the Egyptian one; aired interviews with Israeli officials, which had been taboo; and centered on political matters. Since September 2000, Al-Jazeera provided instant on-the-ground coverage and detailed reports on the latest developments of the Second Intifada.[1]

1. Under the terms of the Oslo Accords (a series of agreements signed beginning September 1993 between the Israeli government of Yitzhak Rabin and Yasser Arafat's Palestinian Liberation Organization), the parties agreed that there would be a transition period of five years (to 1999). After this transition period, a final settlement, concerning borders, Jerusalem, and refugees, would be achieved, and the conflict definitively resolved. The Israeli prime minister was assassinated just two years after Oslo. The difficult transition period stagnated under successive Israeli governments, increasingly dominated by the right-wing, settler-oriented Likud. The transition period came and went. It became clear, in view of settlement activity, the Judaization and colonization of Jerusalem, and the absence of any further Israeli withdrawal, that the dream of Palestinian national self-determination was a mirage. Meantime, the Palestinian Authority (which, under Arafat, had become identical with the PLO, although the latter represented all Palestinians everywhere and the former, only those living in the West Bank and Gaza) was increasingly seen as corrupt, and constituting a new power and economic elite. The failure of the Israel-PLO Camp David negotiations in the summer of 2000 marked the official end of the Oslo era. Demonstrations broke out following a visit by the hawkish Israeli politician Ariel Sharon, guarded by hundreds of armed policemen, to the Dome of

It contributed to circulating images, such as the pictures of the death of Mohamad AlDurra, the Palestinian boy who was shot by Israeli soldiers in Gaza in the arms of his father, stoking the passions of viewers worldwide.

Images circulate locally, too. Under curfew, television becomes a way to see the streets you are forbidden to see. Journalists have special permits and access to places under curfew. On that day, in the living room on the screen, Walid Al-Omary, senior Al-Jazeera correspondent in Ramallah, presented the story of a woman who had a miscarriage waiting at a checkpoint. The story was sensationalist: "This is all that was left of her baby," he said, turning the camera to a puddle of blood. Later, it is through his camera that I learned that the curfew had been lifted and that the streets were starting to fill with people and cars.

Maha's story

When the curfew was lifted for a few hours, I went out to buy groceries. I explained to a shopkeeper what I was studying, and he told me about a woman named Maha who gave birth during the invasion two months earlier.[2] I took her number, called her, and was invited to drink tea within an hour. It was the first story I recorded as part of a project on birth under closure in Palestine.

Maha lived in a cement building typical of buildings built to house villagers who had moved to the outskirts of Ramallah for employment. She had three children and lived in two rooms. She told me the story of her third child's birth.

It was April 14. She had mild contractions. She called her doctor at Red Crescent Hospital and asked him what to do. He said he had been

---

the Rock on September 28, 2000. Israel retaliated with live fire, which resulted in a rising spiral of violence and counterviolence. Within a week, fifty Palestinians were dead, and the second, armed intifada was underway. It lasted until after the death of Yasser Arafat in November 2004, by which time Israel had resumed full-fledged military control of all the West Bank and was preparing its forced withdrawal from the Gaza Strip.

2. All the names of the people I talked with in this book are pseudonyms. I have used the IJMES transliteration system, unless the word is commonly used in romanized Arabic, such as the word *sumud*, for example.

stuck in the hospital, unable to leave for five days now, and that when he gets a chance, he will leave to see his family. He will not wait for the onset of Maha's labor. He told her to get to the hospital if she could, and surely there would be competent people to assist her. But even if Maha could get out of her house, she was afraid to leave her husband and children at home. Her husband was going through a difficult period. He was frustrated from being at home without work and would go crazy if she left the two children with him, not knowing how long she would be away. She thought about it a hundred times before she decided that going to the hospital during the curfew would be a bad idea, even if she could make it there.

She remembered that a gynecologist lived in the new housing complex near her neighborhood. She had been her patient once and still had her number.[3] She called her, and the doctor said that she was at home all the time and was assisting births in a room in her house. So Maha walked to the doctor's home with her neighbor, hiding behind walls and bushes. The doctor told her that she was only dilated two centimeters and was not ready to give birth yet. But Maha insisted that she wanted to give birth because it was risky for her to go back and forth from her home to the doctor's. There were sharpshooters in her neighborhood, and she did not want additional risks. Today she was able to get to the doctor's house. Perhaps that would not be possible tomorrow. The doctor gave her something to speed up the contractions (perhaps oxytocin). She started feeling labor pains, but went home after all and walked around the house. At 6:30 p.m. she went back to the doctor's house. The doctor checked her and told her she would give birth in two or three hours. At 9:00, the contractions had decreased for some reason, so the doctor gave her another dose of oxytocin. By 9:30, she had given birth. The doctor and her neighbor cleaned her up. She had a tear because the delivery was so quick, but the doctor did not stitch her up. Then the doctor started making her feel unwelcome, as if she had another client waiting for her. She told her that her husband was uncomfortable

---

3. It is common for patients to have doctors' cell phone numbers and to use the number for emergencies.

because the room where she assists births is across from their bedroom. She told her that no one sleeps in her house. In proper English (*bil'arabi al-faṣīḥ*, in classical Arabic), she kicked them out. By that time, it was 11:00 p.m. The neighbor had cleaned the baby and wrapped him up so that they could take him out. She told her to gather her strength because it looked like they had to leave. They carried the baby and stepped out.

In the middle of the return route, they heard a tank rolling down the street. They ran to the nearest house and knocked on the door, saying that they were women and needed shelter. The tank was getting closer to them and they were still knocking on the door. Finally, someone opened the door for them. They sat down with them and drank tea, and the lady of the house started saying that she could not believe that the doctor had sent Maha home right after a delivery. And that she had a tear, but the doctor did not stitch her up.

A few hours later, Maha and her neighbor got up to leave again and the young men in the neighborhood called the people living down the street and looked out for tanks from the roof, keeping them on the cell phone. When they got home, the people who had welcomed them in their house called them to say how happy they were to hear that all was well, and they were in the safety of their homes.

But Maha did not feel that comfort in her home for the first few months after the birth. She worried because her husband already had been arrested once and was an anxious person. He did not get involved in politics and feared everything, especially the army. He worried they would come get him again. The children had nightmares about the soldiers coming to the house and taking their father. Maha had to calm everyone down, even though she too was worried and wished she could get out of the house to get a breath of fresh air. When the soldiers had come to their house during her pregnancy, her husband was afraid to open the door for them as they were knocking. She told her husband to open the door before they break it down and start shooting. But her husband was immobilized by fear. So she gathered her courage and went to open the door with her children. The soldier pointed his gun at her, a bit startled at her large belly. He asked everyone to move to one room because they were going to occupy the building for an unlimited period. She felt her feet collapse underneath her from fear, but managed to gather the children and her husband into the room the soldier was pointing to.

When she remembers the anxieties of her pregnancy, she realizes how lucky she was to have had a normal birth.[4] The doctors had predicted she would have complications. For the first three weeks of her pregnancy, she had pain. The doctor asked her to abort. But her brother begged her to postpone that until the end of his wedding celebrations. She prepared and hosted her brother's wedding, which exhausted her. When it was all over, she went to see another doctor, who told her that the heartbeat was normal, the baby seemed healthy, and maybe she did not want to abort. She took that advice.

Months went by. She went back to the hospital for a checkup and the doctor was very worried because she was not gaining enough weight and the fetus was not growing. In twenty days, the fetus would barely gain 100 g/3.5 oz. The doctors predicted that the newborn would need oxygen and would have malformations. They scared her. Every time she went to the doctor, she would vomit. Then she would go to her in-law's house and cry for hours. She wanted a girl so badly, but she was terrified that her daughter would be ill. She went to do the test for malformations (maybe an amniocentesis) and there were no visible problems. She gained a bit of confidence. Through a family member who is active in politics, they contacted Marwan Barghouti.[5] He attempted to influence Red Crescent Hospital to provide her with an incubator, which was costly; it never came through. Her cousins and neighbors lent her money to cover the incubator cost, about 50,000 NIS (about $14,000). But as we know, she never got to the hospital. The day after the baby's birth, the soldiers lifted the curfew for four hours for people to stock up on food. Her husband's aunt took the baby to the pediatrician, who reassured her that the baby was healthy.

4. In Arabic, a normal birth—that is, a vaginal birth with no complications—is referred to as *wilāda tabiʻiyya* (the literal translation is "a natural birth").

5. Marwan Barghouti is a popular leader of the First and Second Intifada. He is an elected member of the Palestinian Legislative Council and the head of Tanzim, the militant wing of the Fatah Party. He is now convicted to life in prison in Israel.

Everyone told her to call her daughter *ijtiyāḥ*, invasion. But a maternal uncle whom she loved and who had recently died had asked her to call the baby Waad, meaning "promise." This had been the name of his beloved. Promise for her was a name that meant a form of hope. So that is the name Maha chose.

Maha thought that her worries would end with the delivery. But during the afterbirth, she felt stir-crazy in the small apartment with her husband, who feared the army would take him away, and the three children who wanted to be outside. She wished she could see her parents, who lived in a neighboring village. She had been counting the days since the last time her mother came to visit her. It had been exactly a month and ten days.

SUMUD

Introduction

Living as Storytelling

Compared with the reality which comes from being seen and
heard, even the greatest forces of intimate life—the passions of the
heart, the thoughts of the mind, the delights of the senses—lead
to an uncertain, shadowy kind of existence unless and until they
are transformed, de-privatized, and de-individualized, as it were,
into a shape to fit them for public appearance. The most current
of such transformations occurs in storytelling and generally in
artistic transposition of individual experiences. But we do not need
the form of the artist to witness this transfiguration. Each time
we talk about things that can be experienced only in privacy or
intimacy, we bring them out into a sphere where they will assume
a kind of reality which, their intensity notwithstanding, they never
could have had before. The presence of others who see what we see
and hear what we hear assures us of the reality of the world and
ourselves . . .
                    —Hannah Arendt (1958) in *The Human Condition*, 50.

In this book, I write about the ways we tell stories about beginnings, as we
try to handle the affects caused by seeing the reduction of the world around
us. As Hannah Arendt describes, we humans both make sense of our experiences and live our experiences by transforming them into stories, by
deploying techniques—storytelling, art, talk, rituals and discourses—to
give meaning to our individual lives. By retelling them, we make them
and ourselves real, alive and recognizable in the eyes of others. We retell
them to adhere to a space where a plurality of people work together to create a world to which we feel we all belong (Arendt 1958, 50–52; Mattingly

1998, 91; Jackson 2002, 12).[1] I have come to think of stories about birth and oral histories in terms of the selective refashioning of experiences to make ourselves alive and part of a world. Yet this appearance is different: it is initiated by all that birth represents, it is part of a relationship between an anthropologist and interlocutor, embedded in a contemporary tradition of oral history in Palestine and it emerges at a particular historical, political, and discursive moment.

Maha's story is about birth in the outskirts of Ramallah under curfew. But the book does not stay in Ramallah or Palestine or with women and their stories about births. It follows connections of meaning. From the stories to the point of experience, mothers, their doctors, their midwives, their nurses, and their families, to the places of birth that take me to cities and hospitals, villages of origin, refugee camps, to Beirut, to Moscow, and to Dearborn. The stories are about human birth under military rule but also about beginnings, the life cycle, steadfastness, connections, continuity, and forms of expression. I write about how people remember social movements that constructed an infrastructure to assist births and how others dissociated from them. It is about birth as a point of contact with Israeli occupation, the Palestinian national movement, state institutions, the hospital, the city, and the law. About how experts must learn new practices and how lay people become experts to assist birth under curfew. Perhaps this is one of the promises of ethnography that Michael M. J. Fischer wrote about in his earlier work on Iran and his later work on science. Thick ethnographic case studies bringing a plurality of perspectives can illuminate processes connecting and transforming individual experiences of people in different places, making them meaningful to a collectivity. Likewise, here, in the end, the stories I tell are about how people want to talk about birth and the capacity to make beginnings.

They are also about the other side of birth, the loss women experience in the after-birth period as they find themselves confined to their homes and villages, longing for relationships with natal families; the exhaustion

---

1. See also Sylvain Perdigon's insightful work on the concepts of appearance, natality, and refugees in Perdigon 2018.

birth attendants experience as they work long hours to assist births and cannot return to their families; the skepticism people express as they observe different kinds of infrastructures, charities, governments, popular movements, and networks that claim to care for mothers; as well as the criticism the poor articulate, pointing to the class-stratified access to medicine. Most importantly, the stories are about a concern for the personal, the human, and the political. The challenge as anthropologist is to mediate and translate, to make visible the ways we come to understand the world around us through multiple media circuits, institutional attention, and cross-cultural perspectives.

Birth is the work of women as they labor and move their babies from the inner worlds of their wombs into an outer world. Doctors, midwives, *dayāt*, technologies, drugs, herbs, prayers, stories, mothers, mothers-in-law, husbands, sisters, other mothers, and neighbors accompany the work of birth. Like Maha, mothers condemned the role of doctors, yet continued to seek their care. They talked to me about birth under closure as the beginning of a life that enclosed them in their villages, neighborhoods, and homes, away from their families of origin. Public culture represents birth as expansion, but mothers spoke to me about birth as isolation, something they thought of as antithetical to growing families. They reflected on loss and being steadfast.

Nurse-midwives often assist birth in Palestine. They experience birth and the closure differently. They were essential to my fieldwork. They took me to the hospital labor rooms to observe births, to their dorm rooms to chat, and to their family homes to spend the day together. They are from poor and underserved rural or refugee families. They migrated to towns and cities, where hospitals are located, often leaving their children, husbands, or parents in villages or camps. Their salaries are essential to sustaining both their families of origin and those by marriage. They work extended hours "like machines," they often said, and long to return to their homes to be with their children or parents. Birth for them is also their *maṣḍar rizq*, their livelihood.

The nurse-midwives urged me to collect oral histories (*tārikh shafawi*). I learned to listen, prompt, and record these long, sustained narratives about the self that begin with a village of origin, work through a middle passage of a life of struggle—in a dispossessed and occupied community, in their workplace and in their homes—and close with an ethically and aesthetically agreeable end, an uncertain future. Guilt and a form of hope emerge in the midst of their narratives as they talk of leaving their children to be raised by others and their parents to be cared for by others, and consciously continue their everyday struggles. They identify *sumud* (steadfastness) as the beginning of their conscious lives, carving a niche for themselves in the national discourse of sumud and refashioning it as a gendered and classed condition of life. The emplotment of their narratives is romantic (White 1979), but with attentive listening and long-term fieldwork, disjunctive stories appear in the midst of their life histories.

Oral history emerged in Palestine in the 1970s as small, decentralized projects, led by scholars, community activists, village councilors and heads of charities. It focused on the testimonies of the Nakba (Catastrophe of 1948), the topography of destroyed villages and rural ways of life, as well as memories of pre-Nakba life. It tells a story of war, displacement, and colonial destruction of culture that constitute central traumatic events of twentieth-century Arab history. While the focus is on 1948 and what existed before, oral history emerges in the wake of the 1967 Arab defeat and Israeli occupation of the West Bank, including East Jerusalem, the Gaza Strip, the Golan Heights, and Sinai. Veena Das (1995) proposes the term "critical event" to describe events that bring into being new modes of action and redefine traditional social categories. A critical event encompasses both world historical processes and the inner life of historical actors. Thus, the accident in the factory owned by a multinational corporation in Bhopal, India, might have been the result of a conjunction of global forces. People, however, did not become conscious of their place in the global order until the industrial accident radically transformed their lives, forcing them to navigate international legal systems and government bureaucracies in order to address the effect of the toxic leak on their bodies. Critical events fundamentally upset existing models of social relations and available categories of conceptual explanation. The overwhelming need to narrativize ultimately impels actors to "invent scripts" (Das 1995, 200). As a result, historical experience transforms culture but also transforms the meanings, purposes, and forms of historical practice.

The 1967 "trauma" of defeat (Jurj Tarabishi, cited in Massad 2007, 18) generated a variety of new forms of historical practice and redefined social categories. Joseph Massad traces the concept of *turāth* (heritage) in Arab intellectual production and identifies 1967 (mirroring the 1798 Napoleonic invasion of Egypt) as a turning point in Arab intellectual production. Most Arab philosophical, political, and psychoanalytic texts from the 1967 period explain the defeat in terms of cultural and psychological tropes about backwardness and arrested development, rather than following a history of capital in the region, as after 1798. At the political level, this is the time period of the shift from Arab to Palestinian nationalism, along with a shift to supporting the Palestinian revolution, with centers first in Amman then in Beirut. Inside the Occupied Territories, the defeat of 1967 and occupation reunited Palestinians in the West Bank and Gaza to the land and people of the areas that had been conquered in 1948, bringing them under Israeli control and subject to Judaization and de-Arabization policies. It also generated an imperative to narrate the Nakba of 1948 using new forms of storytelling, including oral histories.[2]

Unlike the centralized, state-centered oral history projects of newly independent Arab and African countries, the Palestinian oral history experience was a local, decentralized grassroots endeavor, part of what Ahmad Saadi (2006) has called "bottom-up processes, which are generated through localized experiences and institutions" (176), and which are also part of the work of memory that "has been able to save them [Palestinians] from alienation and self-estrangement" (184). Because oral history projects were not produced by a state, there was space for people to appropriate the medium. In the beginning, the practice of oral history involved researchers, who themselves were part of expropriated communities and did what Rosemary Sayigh calls "conservationist" work (2003, 3). They sought to reconstruct destroyed villages through recording oral histories, reconstructing maps, studying the flora, fauna, and geology, as

2. For a rich and detailed attention to the way the Nakba appears in novels, memoirs, photography books, and first-person narratives, and the way it seeps into people's consciousness and their everyday, see Saadi (2002). For other works on remembering the Nakba, see Saadi and Abu-Lughod (2007); Davis (2011); Sanbar (2001); Said (1999).

well as local traditions, sayings, and stories of villages. Thereafter, oral history involved charities, whole villages, and private institutions. It took on a political urgency as oral historians and their teams of interviewers spoke of their documentation as needed for the survival of culture. Indeed, within a decade, the genre of oral history became a known story form and practiced often by oral historians, refugees, and villagers.

More recently, the younger generation, born after the Nakba and the defeat of 1967, often live or work in urban environments and have lived alongside a national movement. There is a shift to narrating an oral history about being a marginalized, struggling, and working person.[3] In a way, the younger generation carved a niche for itself in oral history emphasizing sumud and struggle. In my reading of Adel Yahya's published collections of oral histories (2002), elderly men tell the history of villages, camps, tribes, and states using language that mixes journalism and epic poetry. On the other hand, younger women (under the age of fifty) tell a sustained narrative about the self, with references to dates, massacres, political events, and official mapped places, with a particular emotional tone and force, grieving over the loss of a child and pushing the younger generation to political commitment. I suggest that oral history in the contemporary Occupied Territories is a gendered and classed genre of witnessing in Palestine, often co-produced by young, refugee, and rural, working-class women.

Parts of the shift I observe have been registered by anthropologists inside and outside the Occupied Territories in different ways over time. Rosemary Sayigh noted the difference in narrative genres between elderly and younger women. Elderly, unschooled women told stories (qiṣaṣ) with particular aesthetics and their narratives were characterized by a "hesitancy/plural subject/discontinuity pattern," whereas the pattern of younger women's narrations was "readiness to speak, the singular subject, and autonomous narratives referenced to nationalist history" (Sayigh 1998, 149). Susan Slyomovics (1998) documented the production of the genre of the village memorial book, which is both a literary and an

---

3. A number of researchers have noted the importance of the camp among a younger generation of refugees (Allan 2014; Salih 2018).

ethnographic genre, as well as its relationship to forms of ethnic cleansing. miriam cooke (1987) recorded the gendered differences of stories of the civil war in Beirut. In Diana Allan's ethnography of Shatila refugee camp (2014, 46), she was struck by the "practiced, even stylized" nature of the memories of 1948, while the younger generation of Palestinian refugees who never experienced the Nakba are cautious of the "fetishization of the national entity," and "refuse to inherit the Nakba" (61). Lori Allen (2013) captured the mood of *zahaq*, being "fed-up," and discusses the cynical outlooks of her interlocutors working in the Palestinian human rights organizations that she argues can be a form of awareness and motor for action. Building on these observations in my own work, I heard different segments of society use different narrative forms.

While the nurses and midwives and working-class women told detailed narratives about the self, their brothers and husbands often made short remarks about being fed up. Many were unemployed or had occasional temporary work in construction or agriculture, and most had to live in the circumscribed spaces of their villages or camps. Indeed, the severe closure since the beginning of the Second Intifada in 2000 had gendered effects on the wage labor market, making mobility and therefore employment in certain sectors more difficult for men. Young men rarely volunteered oral history narratives or got excited about my research, as some of the young women from the same families did. In part, this may be because of my being a woman and because they may not have been interested in birth and medicine. But I suggest that it is also because they did not feel that the medium of oral history was theirs to use and that they were isolated and insignificant to the world that I and others were co-constructing in my story.

Paying attention to the forms and genres of stories, and to how they are co-produced, illuminates processes and communities that do not always fit the typical story about Palestine and oral history. This perspective makes certain forms of stories of different segments of society legible or hearable. Following Michael M. J. Fischer's work on life stories and autobiography (1982, 1983, 2003), I trace Palestinian oral history as pieces of historical consciousness, troubled by traces of the other (other human beings, cultural forms, ways of thinking, institutional restructurings,

living beings, and nonliving things and places). Oral history offers the possibility for young working women to narrate a consistent self and history
with a known narrative arc. Ethnographic attention shows how the forms
work, despite the breaks, disjunctive stories, and emotions that complicate
the telling. Furthermore, oral histories always beg the question of what
lives and cultural forms are isolated, erased, and made insignificant by
bringing this narrative to the fore.

From Telling Stories to Making Meaning Local

The purpose of this book is to carefully map the ways in which everyday
people in Palestine tell stories about and experience birth, to bring attention to the forms and genres of stories people tell, and to challenge the
normative site of identity as the location from which to study Palestine.
It consists of two parts. In part 1, I write about oral history and stories—
in this context, the process of narrating a life-changing experience and
co-constructing it into a public story. I begin with the stories of mothers, then move to the oral histories of nurse-midwives. From these diverse
stories, I follow their narratives to larger cultural and political issues: the
effects of the military closure on daily life, colonial dispossession, ethnic
cleansing and its effects on the understanding of work and life, and the
different kinds of services that people are caught up in at the time of birth.
I listen to the ways in which the procedures, rites, and rituals of the hospital makes itself part of oral histories, stories, and inner lives. And from
there, I look into the deployment of the category of *sumud* (steadfastness),
which physicians, midwives, mothers, and their families borrowed from
political culture to discuss different kinds of institutions and conditions
of life. Its semiology became a central thread of my fieldwork and thinking, leading me to different parts of the medical system and to different
spheres of cultural production. I end this part with midwives' use of the
concept of sumud to talk retrospectively about their lives, showing me
their achievements over time. Drawing on my longitudinal work over sixteen years, I trace the ways in which nurse-midwives are upwardly mobile.
They become the first women to own property in their villages, or to move

out of refugee camps and into more expensive parts of the city, and to support their children through university.

The narrative spirals outward from the story of mothers and midwives to stories about the history of the infrastructure of birth in the changing military, administrative, medical, and political context. Doctors were keen on narrating this history in which they played central roles. Nurses and lay people often challenged that narrative to highlight power struggles, class difference, and multiple forms of political action.

In part 2, I follow the history of sumud through the stories about the building of the infrastructure of birth and through my excavation of the concept in cultural life. I trace the beginnings of the use of the concept in poetry and journalism in the Galilee under military rule right after the Nakba. I continue this tracing, from its use to describe the politics of the Palestine Liberation Organization's political program in the Occupied Territories after 1967 to its contemporary deployment by working-class women to describe their conditions of life. Sumud and birth take me to different spheres of the birthing infrastructure, from charitable hospital, to governmental labor room, to village clinic, to the house, the fields, the road, and the phone. Here, I write about the medical setting as a site where procedures, rites, and rituals, led by doctors, nurse-midwives, and family, do the work of accompanying birth and announcing to the birth mother what is happening to her. The birth procedures were similar in all medical settings. Doctors, midwives, and laypeople borrow the concept of "natural childbirth" (*wilāda tabiʿiyya*) from modern obstetrics (Dick-Read 1933) and domesticate it, giving it meanings that make it relevant and familiar in the local context. However, the interviews, observations, and oral histories personalized each birth in its particularities and situated birth in local networks and historical circumstances. I reflect on the new local identity of categories and practices.

The stories people told about the different institutions varied. The medical infrastructure had histories connected to the Palestinian national movement and the struggle against occupation. People remembered and narrated the places and their histories as if they were paying tribute to ancestors of the sites. But some employees and patients re-narrated and reinterpreted these histories to bring out the breaks and fissures of the dominant ancestral story. Thus, I reflect on the meaning of memory and participation.

Telling the Story of the Field

As I write the fieldwork story, I ask where to begin, which stories emerge in my narrative and which ones never appear. As the anthropologist Claude Lévi-Strauss describes at the end of *Tristes Tropiques* (1955), humans live in many worlds at once, some we are in the midst of, and others are in our thoughts. "He [Man] is everywhere at the same time" (Lévi-Strauss 1955, 396). We weave continuity in our lives by giving meaning to experiences closest to us and by denying meaning to those furthest away. This expansion of meaning, brought together through ethnography, is "conducted inwards from without" (396). I have come to think of the process of writing this story as a process of gathering stories and ethnographic material from all around and bringing it inwards, merging it with past and future positions, weaving continuity and meaning to lives, and expanding meaning.

I begin with an arrival scene about curfew and the closure. The fieldwork journey resembled the regular visits I had been taking to see family and friends since I left for university in 1995. Except this time, it was for a long time, my parents would not be present, and my purpose was to do research. Over the years, during my stays, I had observed visible changes in the towns and villages, including new buildings, new forms of police and administrations, new checkpoints, laws, terminologies, dress, consumer goods, political cultures, and especially the restricted access to shared space. For example, hiking in the neighboring hills or swimming in a nearby river was once feasible, but has become difficult or impossible. Since my first research project for an undergraduate thesis, I was troubled, like many observers, poets, and writers, by the reduction of living space and the destruction of lives and cultures that it produced. I was particularly concerned with embodied and health effects.

A focus on childbirth came later, while I was putting together the dissertation research proposal. But birth had been with me my whole life. I think my first memory that I see in the form of photographs before my eyes is of my mother, a midwife by profession, in labor, lying on a wide bed attended to by her midwife colleagues. That was the birth of my brother in a house in Haute Savoie, France, in the winter of 1981. I was three and a half. Thereafter, birth segued itself in and out of my memory with my mother's work as a midwifery instructor and researcher and no longer practitioner, and notably with the story of the breach birth of my second brother in a hospital during a summer vacation in France in 1985. I did not contemplate birth as a research site until I heard a lecture by Rhoda Kanaaneh on her ethnographic work on sexuality, the family, and reproduction among Palestinians in the Galilee. Thereafter, I started to notice how the Palestinian national movement preoccupied itself with birth—in artwork, poetry, speeches, political pamphlets, and health and education policies. But what were the unofficial stories, those not registered by political parties, think tanks, and public art, I thought? And what about women's stories in this discourse?

Probably the book on gendered stories that had the most influence on my thinking at that time was Lila Abu-Lughod's *Veiled Sentiments: Honor and Poetry in a Bedouin Society* (2000). Building on a tradition in the anthropology of Arabia (Meeker 1979; Caton 1990) of collecting, transcribing, and translating thick compendiums of poetry and situating them in the contexts of their telling, alongside a mapping of social institutions, Abu-Lughod's ethnography brought together a body of oral material of Bedouins of the Western desert of Egypt, with an attention to emotion and to women's stories that I felt captured worlds I imagined existed in rural Palestine. Her book also foregrounded moments and modalities of her own experience on the field that to me reflected the potentialities of ethnography.

I began the fieldwork with the story of Maha's birth under closure. But I had come to that interview with a plan to follow the routes of birth stories. Following Michael M. J. Fischer's commitment to thick ethnographies that could eventually add an interpretative layer to sociological analyses and political discourses as a way of cultural critique, I sought to trace capital, politics, and media around birth in as detailed a manner as possible. On the one hand, the interview with Maha took me to her doctor, which took me to the obstetrician who was coordinating a birth network. On the other hand, Maha also showed the way to critiques of medical care and rumors about doctors. From the beginning, the routes of childbirth were leading me to explore various kinds of medical infrastructures, to question the function and meaning of infrastructure, and to pay attention to the formation of social classes.

At the same time, I was part of an intellectual community at MIT that explored the ways science, medicine, and technologies affected modern subjectivities. Joseph Dumit (2004, 2012) wrote about the ways PET scans, drug advertisements, and other medical discourses and practices interpellated subjects who self-fashioned themselves in new ways in American society and how, as a result, the definition of the human was changing. In his work, he was attentive to cultural and political economic analyses of medical categories and diagnoses and the ways they can generate social movements or the ways their lack may generate social formations. It is with his work in mind that I began investigating medical protocols, and handbooks used by medical personnel. I observed practices of births in two hospitals, one in Jerusalem and one in Ramallah, paying attention to the cyborg nature of modern childbearing, medicine as a site of subjectification, and the ways people both embraced and escaped institutional control.

Finally, while I was in the field, Aslihan Sanal (2011) was writing her ethnography of kidney transplantation in Turkey. I visited her, read her writing, and listened to her analyses. She worked with life histories, and using Freud's analysis of mourning and melancholia, analyzed the loss of a loved object, an organ, and the reconstitution of inner lives. She traced the ways loss was mourned and replaced by another object, and in time the person recovered. If the person was not able to replace the loss, then she or he would project feelings for that object upon his or her own ego and sink into melancholy. Like her, I started to hear loss in the birth stories I was listening to, the loss of a part of themselves that they loved, the loss of a relationship to natal families and mothers. I started to listen to the ways in which mothers internalized new relationships and reconstituted inner lives.

In addition to isolation and loss as a site of inquiry, mothers' stories led me to rumors about medical malpractice and the vilification of doctors. Malpractice stories that ended in the birth mother's death were a common story among villagers and townspeople and often targeted particular doctors and hospitals, leading to dismissals and the temporary closing of facilities. Furthermore, mothers' stories had a constant fear as they navigated an underserved infrastructure and poor means of patient transportation due to the closure. But how was conflict resolved? And why did people vilify and idealize doctors at the same time? What routines and rituals did village clinics and hospital labor rooms have in place to protect themselves from the risk of rumors and vilification?

I then started spending three days per week doing participant observation in two hospital labor rooms and taking weekly visits to makeshift birthing clinics in rural areas that I heard about. As the anthropology of birth had traditionally done, I read the routines and procedures of hospital births as rituals that take the birth mother through a rite of passage, sending messages about the new types of relationships she will be experiencing. But while the anthropology of birth has focused on birth as a ritual that deepens institutional and state control over women, I heard the mothers' stories about their experience of birth and the after-birth period as tales of isolation and falling through the cracks of the infrastructure.

The infrastructure had three types of services that people connected to time periods of Palestinian history and the struggle against occupation: what people called the sumud infrastructure of centralized hospitals in urban areas, the popular health movement with a decentralized system of clinics, and the more recent makeshift childbirth network. During my work in the two urban hospitals, doctors, nurse-midwives, and patients referred to the PLO policy of sumud as the main source of funding and organizational force that constructed and maintained this type of infrastructure. They narrated a story about dependency and rent (as the whole of the Palestinian economy is often described by scholars and laypeople alike). But in addition to dependency, they also told a story about local practices of steadfastness in the everyday. From the perspective of women who had given birth, however, the routines and protocols of birth at the hospital marked the beginning of the process that isolated them from their families and communities.

Prominent doctors located in other kinds of institutions, mainly the private sector or the NGO sector, described their work during the 1970s and 1980s as attending to the problem of urban hospitals alienating their patients from their communities. They remembered their work with the mass-based popular health movement fondly. They talked to me of a health and birthing infrastructure that was more participatory and closer to villagers and poor people. In that site, I started to get interested in what participation looked like and what it meant. A group of doctors educated in the former Soviet Union started a health movement that wanted to resist Israeli occupation and break with the tradition of sumud institutions. They referred to themselves as *ṣumūd muqāwim* (resistant sumud) or the popular health movement. They constructed a movement that was different from the model of charitable associations where wealthy notables, businessmen, and states donate to institutions that redistribute to the needy. They saw their work as pushing people to demand health as rights and as addressing class inequalities. The doctors themselves were part of a new class of leaders in Palestine. They were of rural background, although they lived in cities and were educated in the former Soviet Bloc. They started the movement by driving mobile clinics to the villages they were from and then started opening clinics in rural and underserved areas.

Many of the leaders of this movement I knew already. My mother had worked with them for a decade. And both my parents were their friends and colleagues. My parents had arrived in Palestine in 1983, after the Sabra and Shatila massacre, to work in solidarity with Palestinians.[4] My

---

4. In June 1982, Israel launched a massive invasion of Lebanon, intended to drive out the PLO. After three months of sustained bombing and a prolonged siege of Beirut, resulting in almost 20,000 Lebanese and Palestinian deaths, Arafat agreed to evacuate PLO forces to far-flung parts of the Arab world. He demanded and obtained US guarantees that Palestinian civilians would be safe, despite the absence of PLO fighters protecting them. Nonetheless, Israel instructed the Lebanese Falangist militia to enter Shatila refugee camp in Beirut's Sabra neighborhood, and between September 16 and 18, anywhere between 1,000 and 3,500 children, women, and men were massacred, with bright Israeli

father was a historian, educator, and a communist, and my mother a midwife and health researcher. Soon after their arrival, they started cooperating and working with the popular movements, including in the health sector. The popular health movement stories blended with my own vivid memories of their work, as well as with photographs that my parents had taken. I remember both an atmosphere of hard work as well as one of festival, music, and politics, an atmosphere shared with the internationalist cultures of leftist activism of the 1980s. But today, most of the participants in this decentralized infrastructure had dispersed to the private and NGO sectors. They took pride in the movement and criticized it for its shortcomings. My positionality as a researcher, and as someone who grew up and lived in Palestine for most of my life, led me to continuously reflect on change and contextualize my observations and analyses.

Not all doctors who practiced decentralized, barefoot-doctor-type medicine identified with the popular health movement. On the contrary, most of the birth assistants who were part of a childbirth network (doctors and nurse-midwives), made it clear that they were not part of a social movement, that they just assisted births because it was their duty, work, and source of income. They distanced their work and themselves from any political organization. No matter how informal and spontaneous a network is, some find it already too institutionalized and hierarchical. This is a symptom of fatigue and disillusionment with organized political movements.

New mothers were also disillusioned and often critical of the care they received. Some felt mistreated by health professionals, and in particular doctors. They and other community members circulated rumors that transformed themselves into local scandals. These rumors and scandals disrupted the medical infrastructure, at least temporarily, and reiterated communities' demand for better access to medical care.

Birth remained a site of research, although less systematically, for years after I went to the United States to write my dissertation and then

---

flares lighting the alleyways during the two nights of mass murder. An international outcry resulted in the end of the operation.

moved to Lebanon to work in 2007. Through those reflections and a continued questioning of catastrophe, loss, survival, and the need to narrate, I contemplated their longue durée and reinterpreted my corpus of work on storytelling as being about appearances of the living and the ghosts of those who do not appear, who never tell their stories.

PART ONE

Oral History and Stories

1

The Other Side of Birth Stories

In this chapter, I reflect on the genre of birth stories and how to interpret them. I narrate two typical birth stories of rural women who I became friends with during my fieldwork. Inspired by Aslihan Sanal's (2011) ethnography of kidney transplants in Turkey and by the register of the stories themselves, I argue that the stories I collected are about loss, love, and intimacy. Everyday realities like military occupation and border closures are interwoven into birth stories in unexpected, complicated, and ambiguous ways. Indeed, the closure and occupation seep into stories about birth.

Rama's Birth Story

In writing a chapter about birth stories, I think of Rama and Hiba, who mix the registers of military and medical regulations with that of love and loneliness. Both tell anecdotes about love and marriage and both gesture or give clues to the care and love they lost.

I began my fieldwork doing interviews with women who had given birth in villages and towns in the Central West Bank. It worked like this: someone I knew would give me a phone number of a woman who had given birth in her village, and I would call her up and wait for the curfew to be lifted off Ramallah or for the roads to open again (often a few days), and then take the communal taxi to visit the new mother in her home. Some of the women I visited only once, while others I saw on a weekly basis for a year.

I visited Rama in October 2003. Rama, who said she felt more and more anxious, was in her twenties and had three daughters under the age of three. She is from a village west of Ramallah, but upon marriage had moved to her husband's apartment in a nearby village. Her pregnancies were full of anxiety because she never knew whether she would be able to get to the hospital in Ramallah in time for the birth. She prayed that her labor would start on a day when the roads were open and felt lucky because she made it to the hospital for her three births.[1] She delivered the first two babies in a charitable association hospital and her third in the government hospital because her family had become too poor to pay.

Her first child, Myrna, was born with glaucoma (an eye condition), but it was not diagnosed in the newborn, and every year her vision deteriorated. By the time I met her, Myrna was three years old, and the condition had been recently stabilized with eye drops prescribed by an ophthalmologist. Rama was preoccupied by the hourly eye drops and could think of nothing else. She was so obsessed with her firstborn's illness and health, she feared that she was not paying enough attention to her other babies. She worried because they were jealous of the care she gave the first one.

She was at home most of the day caring for her three babies and had little time for anything else. Her mother, who lived on the other side of checkpoints, could not visit often because she cared for her own ill father-in-law. Rama's husband worked in construction all day, and sometimes in the evenings, to make ends meet. She felt lucky that he was even employed, although she had been lonely for three years now since her first birth. In her long days with the children, she wondered whether her husband still loved her the way he did in the beginning. They had met, fallen in love, gotten engaged, directly after which he was arrested by the Israeli army. He was in jail for a year. When he entered prison, he had a leg injury caused by a boulder at a construction site and they feared he would become paralyzed. However, their love for each other grew and his leg healed. He was released and was able to go back to work. Upon his release, they married and had three daughters.

---

1. Numerous cases of births at closed checkpoints of the Israeli military were recorded during the years of the Second Intifada, 2000–2004. According to the Palestinian Ministry of Health, 10 percent of Palestinian women endured labor or childbirth at an Israeli checkpoint between 2000 and 2007, resulting in the deaths of thirty-five babies and five mothers (Powell 2011). See also Shoaibi (2011) and Shalhoub-Kevorkian (2012).

She remembered how, during the birth of her first daughter, she had been afraid for a moment that her husband did not love her from the bottom of his heart. She was in the labor room and there were no other birthing women so the midwives told her she could call her mother to accompany her. She told the midwives that she wanted her husband, so they called him on the hospital loudspeaker. She waited, but he did not come. The midwives said to her, "Why don't we call your mother, because your husband does not love you." Rama cried over this during her labor. But later, her husband appeared, her labor continued, and he accompanied her through birth.

When I walked in to visit her, she spent an hour tidying up the toys, bicycles, balls, blankets, tissues, diapers, spoons, cups, and plates. She had not had a visitor in weeks, she said, and wished her mother could visit her more often so she would feel less alone. Her husband reminded her that she should not feel alone because she spent her days with three children. When they leave, the house will be totally empty for her. The hardest thing in her life has been the illness of her eldest child. She became physically and emotionally exhausted from going through checkpoints to take Myrna to the specialized eye hospital in Jerusalem.[2] She constantly worried that the soldiers would turn her back. They called her a liar, told her that her daughter looked perfectly healthy and that she could take her to the general hospital in Ramallah. But she wanted the best care for her daughter and so she insisted and tried again and again, taking small roads to bypass the checkpoints to get Myrna to the eye hospital. During those times, she would not do housework and she could think of nothing else but those drops she had to put in her daughter's eyes on the hour. She thought of Myrna all the time because she had stopped eating. Her appetite had changed since her eye condition had worsened. She wanted only mother's milk and would be jealous if her mother paid attention to anyone

2. Health institutions in Jerusalem are located on either the eastern (Palestinian) or western (Israeli) side of the city. While Palestinians will sometimes go to the west for specialized treatment, the reverse never happens. The eye hospital is a charitable organization with a long presence in East Jerusalem, operated by the Order of St. John of Jerusalem and servicing thousands of Palestinians from all over the Occupied Territories.

else but her. When Rama first got pregnant with Myrna, she took medication to terminate the pregnancy. She had not wanted that pregnancy, but then she changed her mind and decided to keep the baby. She felt guilty because she could not attend to her other daughters the way she attended to her ill daughter. She said that she tried to treat her other children like Myrna, but it was difficult because of her constant fear that the child might fall ill again, and so she couldn't keep her thoughts away from her. "But if you look closely," she told me, "this other daughter is beautiful, look how clear her eyes are."

The only person she saw was her sister-in-law, Rania (her husband's brother's wife). Rania came to help Rama sometimes and stayed with her daughters when she needed to go to the eye hospital. She listened to Rama. They had become close. She "felt from the heart" with women who went through this loneliness with her. They saw each other during the day. Then at night she felt alone. When she woke up in pain and alone at night, she called her sister-in-law, who calmed her down and, in the morning, came to her place and helped.

After a long visit, I got up to leave. She asked me to stay, and so I stayed for a few more minutes. The children were getting cranky. Rama asked me to come back: "I tell people, I am an orphan, come visit me."

Hiba's Birth Story

I met Hiba on November 9, 2003, during my work at Makassed Hospital in Jerusalem. When she and others registered that day, she agreed I could spend time with her during labor and delivery. She told me that she wanted to discuss my work because she too had gone to university and was interested in intellectual work. She had completed a law degree at Al-Quds University.[3] I told her that I had lots of time and would share my time between her and the other laboring women.

3. There are fourteen universities in Jerusalem, the West Bank, and the Gaza Strip, in addition to an Open University (for continued education) and thirty-eight smaller colleges and community colleges. This may seem excessive for a population of around four million, but it helps to palliate the considerable obstacles placed in the way of mobility by

I walked into Hiba's labor room at the same time as the midwife. Her contractions were still soft. She asked how I spoke such good Arabic and I explained that I had grown up in Ramallah. My parents were foreigners teaching at Birzeit University since 1983, when they came in solidarity with Palestinians. Her doctor had just seen her in his clinic in this hospital and said that she was dilating and that she should not go back to her village because who knows when she could get back to Jerusalem. Her village was not far, and she had a Jerusalem ID (which should give her access to Jerusalem), but you know the closure can cut off anybody anywhere, she told me.[4]

She was afraid. She called her mother who said she was coming, hurrying to the hospital. In the meantime, Hiba had walked into the labor room, taken her veil and shoes off, and sat on the chair. The nurse was preparing oxytocin to speed labor and bring on stronger contractions, but Hiba said she did not want *ṭalq* (oxytocin). The nurse said that she would need it because her contractions were weak and that her labor would take forever if she did not take the IV. "In normal times, you would have gone home," the nurse said. Hiba agreed reluctantly. After a few hours, the contractions were very painful. Her mother had arrived and was holding her hand. Hiba's mother's eyes were welling up with tears, "We have all gone through this, but it is so hard to see your child in pain," she said. She had sneaked juice and biscuits into the hospital, which we all consumed.

---

the occupation. Al-Quds University, with its fifteen thousand undergraduate and graduate students, has a decentralized campus located in and around East Jerusalem.

4. Type of identification card is an essential key to mobility and maintaining residency rights for Palestinians in the Occupied Territories. They range from blue ones (Jerusalemites) to green ones (West Bankers and Gazans). "1948 Palestinians," that is to say, those with Israeli IDs, may, like Jerusalemites, travel freely throughout Israel and the West Bank unless specific closure orders have been decreed. The Gaza Strip is closed to all except Gazans, who may in turn not leave to go anywhere, unless they have been granted specific permission to do so. In theory, Israelis may not enter Area A (under Palestinian Authority control), but the measure does not apply de facto to Palestinian citizens of Israel. Identity cards have been essential to Israel's control of movement and demographics in the Occupied Territories (Tawil-Souri 2012).

Hiba's contractions were getting more painful, but a young doctor making his rounds examined her and said that the labor was not progressing. Hiba was afraid. She was crying. The doctor offered an epidural, but her mother intervened and said the treatment might hurt the mother and baby. Hiba declined the epidural and requested that we tell each other stories (*qiṣaṣ*). In between contractions, she talked about her husband, whom she had met and fallen in love with as she started university. She waited for her husband for years as he finished his medical degree in Russia. Now she was waiting for him to come to the labor room. As she explained this, she took her mother's hand from one side and my hand in the other and she closed her eyes as tears streamed down her face while the contraction passed. She had left a message for him at Red Crescent Hospital in the rural West Bank where he worked. She said to come straight to the labor room, but she had no news from him. Perhaps he had to see so many patients that he did not even have time to check his messages at the front desk. Perhaps he was on a house visit. Perhaps he was at a checkpoint, she wondered. But why could he not call her?

Then she talked about her mother who had come from Beirut, Lebanon. When she fell in love with Hiba's father, she knew that she would go live in his village near Jerusalem and possibly never see her parents and family again. Sure enough, since her marriage to Hiba's father, she had not seen her sisters, brothers, or even her own mother, and had never been back to Lebanon. Sometimes Hiba's mother got to send presents with the few people who could go back and forth (mainly those with more than one passport, in addition to the Palestinian passport.)[5] Every Friday,

---

5. Under the set of agreements beginning in 1994 between Israel and the Palestine Liberation Organization (PLO), West Bankers and Gazans were to be issued with Palestinian passports, subject to Israeli approval of each and every case. These passports are issued by the Palestinian Authority, which exercises limited self-government functions. Sovereign states are free to accept these passports or not. In general, they are recognized, but visa requirements for entry to most countries are restrictive and difficult to obtain. Palestinians spend months, years, or lifetimes trying to obtain a second passport, beginning with a Jordanian one, but preferably one from a European or North American country. These are, on the other hand, not recognized by Israel: if somebody

her mother called one of her family members. Hiba's mother was from a refugee camp in Lebanon, but during the civil war (1975–90), she lived in a beautiful house in Ain Mraisseh (a Beirut neighborhood by the sea), which they had to vacate at the end of the war.[6] She fell in love with Hiba's father, who was a trader, and decided to come to his village near Jerusalem even though she knew she had to say goodbye to her parents and siblings, probably forever. Her mother's move to the village was painful. She was a city woman and she knew nobody. Her husband's village was small and conservative. Neither she, nor anyone in her family in Beirut, fasted during Ramadan. Now, not only did she fast but she also wore the hijab (headscarf), Hiba told me. The hardest was that she missed her mother, Hiba's grandmother, in Beirut. She had thus struggled in her loneliness and brought up a family with love and care. In her own life, Hiba said, her mother was the person who helped her the most. Hiba too had had to struggle. She had to fight to finish her degree. She was pregnant and had to climb up and down mounds, checkpoints, and mountains to get to her university in Jerusalem.

Then her mother told stories about Hiba as a student at Al-Quds University. Hiba was beautiful. She was slim and wore high heels and tight clothes. But she would say, I want to marry the traditional way. Not for love. Because I am afraid of love. I want a husband who will not betray me. Many suitors came to their house asking for her hand, but she refused them all. When Adel appeared, she forgot everything she had said about love and waited years for him while he was in Russia.

Then Hiba, still in labor, continued the stories where her mother had started them, beginning with the sense of sight, similar to many love

---

has a Palestinian passport, he or she is, in the eyes of the Israeli authorities, Palestinian, and nothing else.

6. During the Lebanese Civil War, Beirut was divided into the Muslim west and the Christian east. Early on, most people residing in mixed areas fled to "their" part of the city. Furthermore, thousands upon thousands of people left the country for the duration. Apartments thus vacated were often "squatted" by displaced people from another part of the city or the country. Beginning in 1990, people began moving back to their houses (when these had escaped destruction), and the wartime squatters also moved on.

stories I heard in the field. Adel saw her at her sister's pharmacy and told her he wanted to meet her. They saw each other repeatedly and that is how their love developed. When Hiba fell in love with Adel, her parents did not want him, even though he originally comes from the same village and lived in a neighboring one. His family was too conservative for them. Her mother warned her about marrying into a family that was more religious than her own, but she did not listen. Her fiancé insisted that they could still live the life they wanted, even though his mother and family lived in the same building. In addition, her parents thought he was too quiet: "How will he stand up to your mother-in-law, who will be your neighbor when you move to his house?"

Nevertheless, Hiba said, "We were in love. Like my mother loved my father and married him in spite of being cut off from her family, I loved my husband. Such is love for women. Love for women means loyalty. But you know for men, it is not the same. They are not as loyal, neither to their mothers nor to their wives. While my then-fiancé was in Russia finishing his studies, I was terrified that he would meet another woman. I had nightmares about him meeting a beautiful Russian woman. You know Russian women are beautiful and my husband's friends say that they make good wives because they blend in well with our communities. I was terrified the whole time he was away. The truth is that I am worried about infidelity. I can take many things. But not this. I am not capable of taking that." But she was getting marriage proposals and he was also worried she would accept one. She told him, "Come back soon because everyone is telling me to forget you." That way, she said, she put pressure on him to finish quickly. When he returned, they got married and she got pregnant. The first pregnancy was difficult because she was studying, under pressure to finish her degree, and walking and climbing to get to the university. But her labor started at home and her husband and mother took her to the hospital.

After hours of stories and a labor that I thought could last hours longer, I gave her my number and said I needed to go home because my commute was long. She said she liked me and would call me. The next morning, I called the hospital. The midwives transferred me to the postnatal rooms and Hiba answered, saying she had given birth a half hour after I had left, and that she called her daughter Maram.

Five months later, in March 2004, Hiba called and invited me to her village. I was touched to hear from her and went to see her the next day. She lives in a village in between Ramallah and Jerusalem, both cities I am familiar with, but I realized that I had rarely left the ten-mile stretch of the main road between the two cities. From the moment I stepped out of the collective taxi onto the street of her village, I was surprised to be in an unfamiliar place. A man carrying a little girl greeted me and said he was Hiba's husband, then showed me to their house. They lived on the second floor of a small, new, modern-looking apartment. In the living room, Hiba, her newborn baby, her sister-in-law, and her two children were waiting for me. Hiba's husband disappeared very quickly, confirming her description of him as a shy and quiet man.

I had been recently married, and they took great interest in telling me and teaching me about being a wife and mother. In the midst of their discussions about child rearing, two women, a mother and her daughter, walked in for a visit. Hiba was a bit annoyed that they had interrupted our time together but said they would not take a long time. We all sat and had coffee. Very soon, we learned they had come to announce the daughter was getting married. The daughter explained to us what her life had been like. She was divorced. Her ex-husband let her see her kids only once a week.[7] And each time she gave her kids clothes or presents, their father's new wife would take them away. Sometimes the new wife hit the children. She was so tough with them. Her daughter would come home to her mother with a black eye. "What will come next? Next thing we know, she will only be doing dishes and cleaning." She herself had had a stepmother (her father had remarried). "It is impossible to love them," she said. She was getting remarried, she added, because she knew it would not make any difference regarding how much she could see her children. In any case, she only got to see them once a week. That could not get any worse. Her ex-husband said that he would let her see her children after her marriage,

---

7. Under Sharia law in charge of the personal status law, mothers, unless they have remarried, are granted physical custody of boys until age nine and girls until age eleven (Welchman 2000).

but the children were worried and cried as they were saying goodbye to her for the last time because they thought they would not be allowed to visit her after her marriage.

After they left, Hiba explained that the young woman had loved her neighbor, Ali. She and Ali were inseparable. They were so in love. One day, they had a disagreement, and she left him. Ali became so ill from heartache. People intervened on his behalf and talked to her until she finally agreed to marry him. However, she explained, "His manhood was hurt. He could not take it. They had two children, but he created many problems. He is a complicated man. He was bitter and getting his revenge for her having rejected him in the beginning. He would beat her. Therefore, they got a divorce. Since then, it has been horrible. She has had many suitors since then, about four or five. She and the suitor would like each other and get engaged. But Ali would intervene before the marriage. He would talk to the suitor and tell him that she is not a good person. He would convince him not to marry. It is good this time she is getting married," Hiba said, "but she could have made a much better match if it were not for Ali's interventions."

Naela, Hiba's sister-in-law, explained that when children are involved, so much is at stake. They become your heart, your body, your life. You realize that after you give birth. You become so much stronger and richer, and yet so much more fragile. You can be broken. She realized after the birth of her firstborn, Mohammad, how much she missed her life as a little girl with her mother and father. Her father used to feed her pieces of barbecued chicken with his own hands and still does when she visits him. In the summer afternoon, he would wash the fruit and bring it to their large veranda where they would sit together and savor the sweetness. She was from one of the richest families in the village. Her father owned a large house on the top of the village. She was the only girl and her father's favorite. Her husband was not rich, but he was educated. He was a pharmacist. Naela had married in her late teens, had moved to her husband's house across from her mother-in-law's house, and had two boys. Her life after the births became difficult, she said. Her husband did not help her at home. She cleaned, cooked, fed the children, and put them to sleep. She missed her parents, but she cherished her new family as well. Her two children were the center of her life, and she and Hiba had become very close. They felt like they now shared a life.

I got my things ready to go home because I wanted to pass the main checkpoint before nightfall. Hiba's husband said he would drive me to the checkpoint. We had barely driven a few minutes when we found ourselves in front of a *ṭayyār* (flying) checkpoint, not a regular one, a temporary one that can appear at any turn in the street. Hiba's husband opened his window and said in Russian that he was a doctor and was just driving me to the main checkpoint. The soldier said that it was a completely closed area and there was no way anyone would get out of the village. I handed him my passport and told him I had been on a visit for a few hours and wanted to go sleep in my own house. He shouted that it was no use talking to him or waiting here, that everyone should go home because there would be no way out until tomorrow. We turned around and tried another road out of the village, but there was a checkpoint there and dozens of cars trying to get out on the same road. We drove back to their home, where the husband said he would leave us to be comfortable and that he would sleep at his mother's house across the street. The next morning, we got up early and Hiba's husband drove me to the main checkpoint on his way to work. The road was completely open, as if there had never been Israeli vehicles, checkpoints, and dozens of cars waiting to travel the night before.

Birth, Loss, and Love

I met new mothers throughout my fieldwork years and learned from them what it meant to have given birth recently, with a sense of self that was changed. In rituals and popular culture, births celebrate a new life that women bring from inside their womb to outside of it. For the mother, people celebrate it as a moment when women grow a new intimate relationship with a child and a new identity as a mother. The folklore of birth involves gift giving, ululations, and passing out sweets. Documented stories in the media about birth at checkpoints or under siege have redemptive and romantic endings. What I heard from new mothers, however, was rarely a story of enrichment and growth, but usually one of loss. With the birth of a baby, new mothers felt like they had lost relationships with parents. They longed for their support and love, which they often could not receive because families were separated by checkpoints and husbands did not fulfill that purpose. Palestinian women rely largely on their mothers and family members, rather than professionals or self-help guides, in learning about childbirth, newborns, and childcare. This may, upon separation, accentuate their loneliness.

In the United States, postpartum depression has become the common way to understand feelings of distress after childbirth. In her book, Verta Taylor (1996, 32) tells the story of how, starting in the 1980s, women started turning to psychiatry and self-help literature to understand and manage their feelings of distress after birth. In the United States, the main sources of socialization into motherhood are books, magazines, friends, and childbirth education courses (37). Indeed, Taylor argues that women were active participants in drawing on medicine, psychiatry, and self-help literature to frame their feelings of guilt, anxiety, depression, and anger. In Palestine, on the other hand, mothers and mothers-in-law were central to new mothers' learning about birth. Furthermore, they understood their loneliness after birth as a social and political problem that had to do with the nature of contemporary families and the way the closure was separating family members from each other.

The anthropology of birth (Martin 1987; Davis-Floyd 1992) has focused on the gradual medicalization of reproduction. Some have analyzed the ways in which the Western biomedical model disempowers pregnant and birthing women by symbolically and physically constructing them as weak and in need of help from doctors and medical institutions. Others have focused on the ways women in labor are treated disrespectfully or like ill patients, requiring them to give birth in the lithotomy position or with interventionist methods and disregard for the caring and support needed during childbirth, what scholars in Latin America have called "obstetric violence" (Williams 2018; Sadler 2016). This literature resonates with many stories I heard about medical practices at birth and some of their traumatic effects. Nevertheless, I felt there was in addition something fundamental about the stories of sadness I heard, which were telling of abrupt loss of care and love and adapting to a more lonely life, isolated from long-term relationships.

Loneliness has long been a matter of social scientific interest. Emile Durkheim (1951) employed the concept of anomie to understand some of the shifts he was observing in industrializing urban centers. He argued that such societies were not providing people with moral guidance, integration, and social interaction and this disruption led to the condition of anomie. At the individual level, anomie is characterized by social mal-integration, feelings of alienation, helplessness, and loneliness. The social sciences often connect anomie to European city life, the importance of individualism, and the generational shift to smaller families. But there is also a type of isolation and loneliness that emerges from experiences of exile, displacement, separation, and the imposition of militarized borders and immigration laws that may not have the same genealogy.

Indeed, feeling isolated and lonely has become a common condition for people worldwide, as military, economic, and environmental catastrophes have displaced people in unprecedented dimensions. Borders, camps, and immigration laws separate displaced people from family and familiar relationships. Various media, opinion pieces, films, and memoirs document experiences of deep loss and loneliness (Oliveira 2018; Stringer 2018). Thus, retelling these stories from rural Palestine is important because it is relevant to the condition of millions in the region, and the world, and reflects a type of experience that cannot be explained only by connections to industrialization, modernization, and urbanization.

The stories of loneliness are intertwined with the history of the shift to wage labor and the change in the structure of families from extended to nuclear ones.[8] These shifts have changed motherhood, shifting childcare responsibilities to the mother, including the responsibility to educate children. Yet, the stories of loneliness here are also embedded in the context of restrictions on rights and mobility in Palestine. At birth, new mothers

8. The literature on the shift to wage labor and its effects on families and gender relations is rich. See, for example, Collier (1986) for work on the remaking of families and womanhood in a Spanish village.

are stepping into a life with a baby who is entirely dependent and with few people around to support them. Those who are there, husbands, neighbors, or in-laws, are often new to them.

The mothers feel lonely and isolated in the village and house. Rama, for example, explained that she would wake up at night unable to sleep because of her fear of being alone. "I am an orphan," she said to me as I was about to leave from my first visit to her. Another new mother, Ola, said she cried every night when everyone was asleep for the first few months after giving birth because she felt alone. She longed for her mother's love and support. Birth reorganized social relations that were decades old for these women. For example, they were no longer in close living quarters with their siblings and parents and could not visit them often.

In their new villages and towns, they were considered *gharība*, or foreign, even months and years after they had moved there.[9] However, slowly over time, they constituted new relationships with their sisters-in-law, husbands, other in-laws, or neighbors, which helped them cope with their loneliness. Sometimes, because of the illness of a child, loss of household income, or abusive relationships, for example, they never acclimated to their new lives. Some had harrowing stories of discovering they were in an abusive marriage, struggling for years to get a divorce, and sometimes being separated from their children for years. These women often lived in their parents' homes and talked about things spiraling out of control, crying every day, not sleeping, having to leave work, and then suffering from having no income. They encountered unexpected emotions and were unable to feel settled. New mothers needed to develop new tactics, each doing so individually according to her unique past and life history (Wick 2011). Through the changing nature of things before and after birth, they discovered that their lives were enclosed in many ways. Their stories about loss of relationships and love are also indicative of the political world around them, with closures, economic hardship, and a land chopped up by checkpoints and unequal access to care. Indeed, they were

---

9. See Abou Tabickh (2010, 2012) for attention to women's migration to their husband's villages and the way villagers consider them "gharība."

isolated by closures that made family members' mobility difficult and they were enclosed within their new families with husbands and in-laws who did not compensate for the love and care they lost.

I was not expecting to hear about loneliness and longing for love in the stories. I was expecting birth to be about the celebration of new life and to be part of the public discourse about having babies as a tactic of Palestinian resistance. Since Israel's founding, the determination to make it a Jewish state led to such policies as budget allocations, health insurance, and medical services to encourage Jewish Israelis to reproduce, while at the same time discouraging Palestinian births (Kanaaneh 2002; Fargues 2000). For its part, the Palestinian national movement considered having babies a means of resistance to Israeli hegemony (Kanaaneh 2002). Furthermore, many men and women bring up housework and childcare as part of the work of *sumud* (steadfastness), part of the everyday tactics to raise young men and women for Palestinian resistance (Peteet 1991). Poster art, leaflets, and public speeches are full of images of women birthing and raising the children of the revolution.[10] Yet here, as both Rama and Hiba's narratives show, new mothers' narratives were largely depoliticized and denationalized. Rare were the allusions to the resistance movement. Discussions of everyday tactics of resistance to Israeli occupation revolved around surviving the closure in its different forms. Closure represented a barrier to getting to and from hospitals and clinics in cities and a cause for the interruption of normal social life and, in particular, the limitation of social relations with family members in other villages. In the after-birth period, the new mother becomes enclosed and depoliticized.

The depoliticized and denationalized narratives are characteristic of a broader mood among Palestinians at the time of fieldwork. The end of the Second Intifada (2002–6) was a time of exhaustion with the Palestinian authority and political parties, and a deflating of the national project in general. Lori Allen (2013) diagnosed the mood of the time as being

---

10. For examples of poster art, see *The Palestine Poster Project Archives. The Liberation Graphics Collection of Palestine Posters*, https://www.palestineposterproject.org/artist/115 /poster-imaged-full. For an analysis of Palestinian art, see Boullata (2009); Scheid (2013); Toukan (2021).

best named by the feeling of "zahaq" (being fed up). Had I done field-work in the 1980s, the narratives would have been different. They prob-ably would have been much more in tune with the discourse of political parties and the Palestinian Authority. Thus, I heard women's narratives of loss and loneliness as part of a general shift toward expressing exhaus-tion with the projects of political parties and with the nationalist project more generally.

I tried to understand the worlds of my interlocutors as anthropolo-gists have done before me. Much of the anthropology of birth and mater-nal health understands the history as one of gradual medicalization and disempowerment of women. Robbie Davis-Floyd's (1992) landmark work, *Birth as an American Rite of Passage*, emphasizes the ways in which medi-cal and technological births in the United States are rites of passage. Hos-pital rituals take the birth mother through phases that initiate her to a new status as mother and reinforce the medical institutions' control over their bodies and families. The stories Davis-Floyd co-produced with her inter-locutors concerned a feeling that the state and technocracy were increas-ingly in control of bodies and subjectivities. The narratives of new mothers in my work, on the other hand, focused on being isolated and enclosed in their homes. Many showed their need for access to medical institutions, and especially for mobility and contact with people and relatives.

Most of the mothers wanted to talk with and befriend me. In fact, many first interviews concluded with a request from the mother to return for a follow-up visit. As one birth mother put it upon my departure: "Do it again. Next time, without your study, come back, we can talk again." Wanting to talk to me had to do in part with my positionality on the field: I was a woman researcher; I spoke in a familiar central West Bank dialect; I was clearly familiar with social life and everyday politics. Yet, I was not kin; I was not from a Palestinian family; I was also foreign. In addition, the desire that I come back was a symptom of their loneliness.[11] Like Rama and Hiba, many remember feeling fear during labor that their husbands did not love them and that their parents and siblings loved them in ways

---

11. For an insightful perspective on wanting to talk, see Elizabeth Saleh (2017).

that husbands did not. With time, many cultivated relationships with sisters-in-law, in partial replacement of the love they felt for their own sisters and mothers. Gradually, some relationships with sisters-in-law and neighbors alleviated their loneliness and isolation.

In Palestine studies, an interpretation focused on loneliness and love might be regarded with skepticism, as it seems to depoliticize Palestinian lives. I explore here the interwoven nature of intimacy, military occupation, and politics in the lives of young, rural Palestinian women in the Central West Bank. By putting birth stories at the center of my analysis, and because birth is a rite of passage for the recruitment of new family members, I revisit the meaning and function of family and marriage in Palestinian society. It risks provoking suspicions of depoliticizing the Palestinian family, as if a story of Palestine and family must always return to the ethnic and traditional belonging and show either resistance to or complacency with colonialism. Such a perspective assumes that family and social relations are divorced from the political subjectivity of people with rights in the modern world. But it is the political imaginary, which is distributing and structuring rights through populations at the global, territorial, local, and domestic levels, that constitutes the background for this chapter.

In 1991 the Israeli military instituted the closure policy, which refers to Israeli restrictions on the movement of Palestinian goods, labor, and people, first of all into Jerusalem. Gradually, restrictions were imposed on movement between the Gaza Strip and the West Bank, and between them and Israel. Since 2000, restrictions on mobility separate regions, cities, and villages from each other. The policy of the closure works at multiple levels (Peteet 2017, 11; Halper 1999). The first level involves the control of space through the location of Jewish colonies and their bypass roads, military bases, checkpoints, and closed military areas.[12] It includes land grabbing, counterinsurgency methods, and a general carceral politics constraining

---

12. Literature and films depict everyday experiences in and around checkpoints, including Hammami (2004, 2010); Tawil-Souri (2009); Elia Suleiman's 2002 film, *Divine Intervention*; and Hani Abou Assad's 2002 film, *Rana's Wedding: Another Day in Jerusalem*.

mobility. The second layer is bureaucratic and legal, involving permit and planning systems, with a set of restrictions that severely constrain Palestinian mobility and limit construction. The closure is buttressed by a hierarchy of identification cards, giving different rights to mobility: Jerusalem IDs have the most rights; then come West Bank IDs, with different rules for mobility depending on place of birth and residence; and then finally Gaza IDs, with maximum restrictions.[13] Under the closure system, people are assigned to specific spaces and constrained in their access to others.

The closure marks the continuation of colonial settlement policies that started in 1948 with the expulsion from Mandate Palestine of 750,000 Palestinians to create the state of Israel. The remaining Palestinian Arab population was placed under military occupation from 1948 to 1966. One year later, in 1967, Israel occupied the West Bank, Gaza Strip, and the Sinai Desert, sharply limiting movement across the borders of Jordan and Egypt for Palestinians. That year, Israel reopened borders with the rest of Palestine, the territories conquered by Israel in 1948. While the occupation of 1967 closed the West Bank off from neighboring countries, such as Jordan, it reopened the borders between the West Bank and 1948 Israel. Finally, beginning in 1991, after the First Intifada and at the beginning of negotiations between the Palestinians and Israel, the closure gradually came into being.[14]

---

13. See Helga Tawil-Souri (2011) for an analysis of the politics and materiality of ID cards. She traces the history and use of the ID card in Israel and the Occupied Territories and explores the ways in which the ID cards provide a low-tech, visible, and tactile means of power, distinguishing hierarchies by means of color (green ID for West Bankers, orange for Gaza IDs, and blue for Jerusalem and Israeli IDs); by language (Hebrew, Arabic, and Hebrew); and with the category "nationality" (Jew, Arab, Druze, or Bedouin).

14. The First Intifada, or so-called revolution of the stones, broke out in Jabalia refugee camp, the largest one in Gaza, and quickly spread to the rest of the Occupied Territories. It was a mass movement. Within months, Israel and the international community had accepted that there would have to be changes made to the status of the Palestinians. For work on the First Intifada, see Heacock and Nassar (1990). The contributions for this edited book were written by scholars in Palestine (mainly Birzeit University professors) during the uprising. For other works, see Lockman and Beinin (1989); Schiff and Yaari (1990); and Heacock and Jradat (2020).

Anthropologist Lori Allen (2008) identified Israeli settler colonialism as a form of colonialism implemented through technological prowess, military expertise, brute force, and overwhelming physical control. It is devoid of the "mission civilisatrice" of European colonialism, which understood itself as having a mission to change native subjectivities. Allen argues that such a form of colonialism, uninterested in molding Palestinian subjects, shapes the ways Palestinians respond to occupation, a mode of acting she calls "getting by." Neither being complacent nor resisting, it denies the very logic of occupation by simply managing life as the pressures of enclosure inexorably mount.

In my work, typical birth stories often morph into stories of love and intimacy and a sense of malaise and fear of losing relations because of the curtailment of mobility and of arrested life trajectories and unequal rights. What I hear are accounts of love and loneliness, as well as hints and clues about fears of making visible the intimate relationships between parents and children, between spouses, and between sisters-in-law. I interpret the denationalized and depoliticized narratives of malaise and anxiety as expressing how "getting by" (Allen 2008) takes a toll on well-being. Indeed, neither being complacent nor resisting occupation, just managing everyday life under the regime of restrictions of citizenship and mobility rights, an organic part of a historical process of settler colonial policies, profoundly affects family relations. In villages, survival often depends on family relations as well as the meaning and expression of lost intimacy and love. While active resistance often brings with it destructive and tragic consequences (such as bullet injuries, martyrdom, home demolition, torture or long-term imprisonment), just "getting by" has more subtle yet exhausting consequences. The denationalized malaise and anxiety women express about love and birth contrast with the notions of politics, resistance, identity, negotiations, and strategies, which blind us to the sneaky violence that the distribution of rights exercises on the fabric of intimacy.[15] Indeed, Nahla Abdo (2011) has shown that to understand

15. There are a number of insightful recent works on living with protracted violence in Lebanon and Palestine and the ways in which it manifests itself on relationships and inner lives. See Al-Masri (2017); Feldman (2015); Giacaman et al. (2011);

gendered experiences and women's lived realities, it is important to un-veil the way the Israeli state (and in particular, its control over access to land) shapes the construction of classed and gendered experience. Abdo (2011) focuses on institutional state practices and the history of the dis-possession of Palestinians and the ways it limits Palestinians' citizenship and mobility rights, as well as the ways it shapes gendered experiences of housing, living arrangements, and employment. Furthermore, recent ethnographies of transnational migration and parenting have emphasized the impact of migration decisions and citizenship on the work of mother-ing and on the trajectories of and emotional toll on children and parents (Oliveira 2018; Perrenas 2001).[16] Indeed, the distribution of citizenship, mobility, and property rights shapes marriage, family, and intimate rela-tions. This is often erased by the compartmentalization of the political, with its violent history, and the personal and familial (often a protected space, sometimes politicized as a site of everyday resistance).

Fieldwork has shown that the worries about what is political and oppositional rarely emerge in conversations with new mothers. The more familiar I became with my interlocutors, the more my infrequent ques-tions on such topics were received with polite fatigue. They would give me a look I interpreted as boredom or make a cynical joke about politics and move on to another subject, as if telling me that I should be more aware by now, as if these words had lost their evocative power. By contrast, conversations about love and the family were taken up with powerful and passionate discussion. Nevertheless, numerous interlocutors, both men and women, had participated in demonstrations, and been wounded or imprisoned, and some had worked closely with a political party from a young age. Thus, politics and opposition to Israeli occupation had also been an ever-present aspect of their lives. These women, then, avoided talk about the political; I discovered from them only later that they had fully participated in public political activities over the years. This suggests that

---

Meari (2014a); Hage (1996); Hermez (2017); Khayyat (2020); Moghnieh (2021); Obeid (2019); and Segal (2016).

16. See Elizabeth Saleh's (2016, 2018) work on childhood, labor, and migration in Lebanon.

political participation, resistance, and identity don't overshadow all other analytic categories.

I am reluctant to use the concept of the oppositional practices of everyday life, a dominant framework in understanding women's subjectivity in the social sciences. Saba Mahmood (2005, 33) argued that this focus on resistance in gender studies is connected to a particular genealogy in the literature, anchored in the autonomous liberal individual, who is always wondering whether he or she is acting morally and against oppressive regimes. This history, she argues, does not apply to the Egyptian pious women she worked with. They had a different notion of agency. Following Mahmood and others such as Elizabeth Povinelli, I am less interested in the hidden politics of ordinary life and more in the kinds of subjects produced by historically contingent arrangements of power.

Narrating the self and practices of self-making thus take on new political relevance, delinked from the goals of progressive politics. Indeed, giving birth is as transformative as joining political parties and working in public politics, and often more so. The strategies women use to cultivate new relationships and selves in a new location were efficacious for shaping and constituting the individual. Such strategies included forging relationships with sisters-in-law or neighbors and examining their own experiences with them and with me.

These observations align with Suad Joseph's insights on constituting selves in the Arab world. She discusses "patriarchal connectivity" as an important process in "selving" (1999, 12). By connectivity, she means relationships in which a person's boundaries are relatively fluid, so they feel part of significant others. Persons do not experience themselves as only bounded, separate, and autonomous (12). Maturity is signaled in part by the successful enactment of myriad connective relationships. This type of connectivity privileges males and seniors and mobilizes kinship structures, morality, and idioms to legitimate and institutionalize gendered and aged domination.

Connectivity is particularly visible for Joseph (1994) at puberty, where young women and men see themselves as extensions of parents, brothers, and sisters. Brothers are privileged to enter the boundary of the self of others, shape its contours, and direct its relationships. They show both love and control through everyday practices of supervising where their teenage sisters go and what they wear as well as dancing with and caring for them. The connective patriarch sees his sister as an extension of himself. He may speak for her, make decisions for her, and read and expect to be read by her. In other words, people are summoned to recognize themselves through relationships with siblings and families of descent. I suggest that birth is another moment when patriarchal connectivity is particularly visible. In the context of the closure, where mobility between villages is restricted, young women who can no longer visit with their families of origin experience the transition as disorienting and sometimes as a shock. It is a formative moment for them and, with time, they slowly reconstitute themselves and their connections with new family members, such as in-laws, husbands, and neighbors.

In Aslihan Sanal's ethnography of kidney transplantation in Turkey (2011), she draws on life histories to analyze the loss of a kidney as a loved object, demonstrating the ways patients reconstituted their lives after the transplant. She traces how loss was often mourned and replaced by another object and, in time, the person recovered. After my initial surprise to be collecting tales of loneliness and longing during narratives of childbirth and new motherhood, I started to hear loss in the birth stories. The life stories I recorded seemed similar to Sanal's (2011) about the loss of an organ. In a way, it seemed that women who had given birth had lost an organic piece of themselves, a part that they loved. From Rama, Hiba, and others, I learned to listen to birth stories as stories of abrupt loss of women's relationships with their parents, mothers in particular. They were abrupt breaks with their past. Then I listened to the ways in which new mothers internalized new relationships with husbands, sisters-in-law, neighbors, and mothers-in-law and reconstituted their inner lives. Hiba, for example, noted that the closest person to her was her husband's brother's wife, who lived downstairs. She was uneducated and came from a village farther away, near Nablus, but she was the only person with whom Hiba conversed daily. In the social sciences, when birth is connected to kinship, it is a practice of "kin-work" (di Leonardo 1987, 442–43), a mode of recruiting, maintaining family members and expanding kin. But the new mothers in occupied Palestine were experiencing it as a reduction of the world and relations around them. The process of loss at birth was one that, while intermeshed with politics, was depoliticized. Talk was about love, courting, engagement, marriage, and parental love and its loss.

While new mothers mourned the loss of their relationships to family, they recovered from birth and worried about the care of their babies and, as they did so, other relationships became significant to their lives. Drawing connections between biological reproduction and sociality, new mothers spoke to me of their new lives by narrating birth stories. They spoke to me of labor rooms, home births, fights to get through to the clinic, and anxieties of being alone. Through their stories, I understood how they felt changed by things external to their wills, but which became part of them.

Where birth stories may be about the failures of the state and class-divided medical care, they are also about new kinds of family ties. This period of the first year after birth seems to be a potentially vulnerable moment in women's lives when they feel isolated. It is an intense meaning-making period when they must care for their baby and make sense of new family dynamics. With time, they make their loneliness livable by finding support from women who live close by.

Contact with medical institutions at birth were part of the story too. New mothers described their new realities to me in stories about situations they had encountered during labor and delivery. They spoke of access to the hospital, restrictions on mobility, hospital care, side effects of drugs, searching for money to pay bills, family dramas, and social pressure. They had to make their lives their own again after unfamiliar situations that had unexpected effects and emotions.

On the one hand, there were trends regarding the process of giving birth that could be understood in terms of oppositional practices of everyday life. Interlocutors spoke of birth and marriage that involved passing through checkpoints legally or illegally and sometimes crossing borders. Some interlocutors arranged to give birth in the United States with relatives to acquire US citizenship for the newborn. Others married someone they knew living in the Gulf and joined wealthier in-laws. Still other interlocutors defied Israeli mobility and transmittance of identity cards laws. For example, pregnant women with Jerusalem identity cards gave birth and lived in annexed Jerusalem, often separated from their spouses, in the hopes of managing to have their newborns acquire and keep a Jerusalem ID. In most cases, birth involved crossing checkpoints or taking back roads to receive care in hospitals.

Sometimes families named their newborns to evoke Palestine, resistance, and destroyed villages, with names such as Filastin (Palestine), Jenine (a West Bank city) or Intissar (meaning "victory"). These stories highlight how birth (and marriage) are important to defiant politics and national belonging. They refer to enduring communities of belonging, national, familial, village of origin and neighborhood. They also refer to birth in the form of enduring ways of life, "we give birth this way," for example, to talk about particular practices, like coming to the hospital at the last minute of labor. These practices are shunned by modern medicine, but there is a sense of pride and defiance when women refer to these practices. The stories offer proof that occupation produces different tactics, individual and collective, to reconquer people's rights and silence their biopolitical status as occupied and stateless people. In fact, birth itself, since the 1950s at least, has become a practice often thought of as oppositional and political (Kanaaneh 2002).

On the other hand, I am hesitant to claim these stories as proof that birth is political. By political, I refer to deliberate procedures to highlight community belonging or that are part of the struggle to regain rights. I have never heard my interlocutors talk of marriage or birth in those terms, nor have I heard them denigrate any kind of birth that is not thought of as political. On the contrary, when I referred to a practice I thought of as political, such as naming practices, interlocutors responded less in the register of politics and more with narratives of love and care, love for their children and husbands, and worries about loss of love.

The preeminence of the motif of love in discourse about birth shows a specific definition of intimacy that centers on repeated encounters and "getting to know" someone. This became particularly clear when I asked interlocutors how they met their husband or when I would ask, "What counts as love?" Hiba's husband-to-be, for example, saw her at her sister's pharmacy in a neighboring village, and then they arranged to meet multiple times. The repeated encounters emerge from legal, social, and medical regulations that people endure or from the material and affective dynamics that are artifacts of such encounters. They are neither explained through the foundational event of romantic love or individual freedom, nor by the categories of social constraint and arrangement (Tekce 2004; Povinelli 2006). Furthermore, what these stories tell is not about intimate relations founded on events of falling in love bringing out individualities from the places and belongings in which they are embedded (Povinelli 2006).

A poignant example of the ways in which legal and social barriers shape encounters and relationships is the case of Lamis. She was originally from Gaza but had a West Bank ID because her family had emigrated to a village near Ramallah before 1967; she was registered as a West Banker by the Israeli authorities. She married a maternal cousin who was a "returnee," meaning he had returned to the West Bank with the Palestinian Authority in 1994. He saw her in her family home, and they started meeting regularly; then they got engaged and married. Due to a change of work about six months later, he moved to Gaza, the original place of residence of their shared family.

Lamis moved to Gaza for a month to live with him there but could not find work and was disturbed by living conditions. She moved back to her village in the West Bank. They divorced before she gave birth to their daughter. Her daughter has never seen her father because Gazans are not allowed to go to the West Bank except on special work contracts with the Palestinian Authority, which her ex-husband no longer had. Lamis facilitates a Skype call between her ex-husband and her daughter every evening.

When I mentioned to Lamis the amazing work she puts into networking between her ex-husband and her daughter, and that I thought it was political, in defiance of the restrictions on mobility, she shrugged the comment off and emphasized the loss she felt for herself and for her daughter. Thus, the stories are about encounters and getting to know each other in the grid of legal restrictions on mobility and residency rights. Furthermore, they are about a certain sadness of losing relationships amidst legal and mobility restrictions. In fact, when I asked Lamis to give an account of what she was doing in terms of the discursive division between politics and the personal (networking between her ex-husband and her daughter was in defiance of restrictions on mobility, I said), she avoided the language of politics and pointed to sadness because of loss and the importance of care, obligation, and love, such as arranging Skype calls. Emotions and gestures of care were important in many other stories too, such as having people nearby during birth (in Rama's and Hiba's stories, for example), or to parents feeding their adult children with their hands (as in Hiba's story), or feeling fear during labor that their husbands might not love them. These personal anecdotes regarding care and love seem to be more important than what is political or nonpolitical, and yet deeply connected to the political and to the distribution of rights.

Since women's birth stories often shifted to love and marriage, they showed the terminologies, ethics, and plots thereof. Often, men and women know of each other beforehand, as young people of the same generation and from the same or neighboring villages. Love starts with the man seeing the woman. Then the woman sees the man repeatedly. Then they get engaged and hold the legal marriage, *katb ktāb*, and finally they end with a public ceremony, the wedding. After the wedding ceremony, the bride symbolically, and often physically, goes to the groom's village and house. As Hiba highlighted in her stories, the norm is patrilocal marriage, with the wife moving to the husband's village, neighborhood, or living quarters. And, therefore, the closer the groom is physically and culturally, the closer the bride can be to her parents.

Normative elements of marriages and families have long occupied specialists of the Middle East: the preferential treatment of communities of origin, endogamy, wives moving to husband's locality, patrilocality, and the importance of families of descent.[17] The stories of birth and marriage I collected show the durable aspect of some of these normative practices.[18] The closure made patrilocality worrisome for many families, as visits between families of origin and daughters became difficult. It reinforced

17. For work on various aspects of marriage, patrilocality, and endogamy in the Middle East see Granqvist (1931); Hildred Geertz (1979); Khuri (1975); Kandiyoti (1988); Sholkamy (2003); Abou-Tabickh (2012); Perdigon (2008).

18. Penny Johnson (2006) shows through surveys and analyses that many marriages are endogamous in Palestinian society of the West Bank and Gaza. She analyzes these marriage practices as strategies by both men and women to maintain "closeness" as a form of security and development in an insecure environment.

a type of gendered loneliness where women felt they had little support because their parents could not visit them often.[19]

But my fieldwork showed that patrilocality is complicated, ambiguous, and not always the way new spouses locate their homes. Sometimes, as in the case of some of the midwives, husbands would move to the wives' villages because of support they got from the wives' parents and sisters, in terms of both living space and help in raising children. Sometimes, too, couples moved to wives' neighborhoods or villages so their children could get specific types of IDs. For example, many families who had one parent with a Jerusalem ID would move to Kufr Aqab, which is near Ramallah but annexed by the Israeli Jerusalem municipality. Or sometimes husband and wife would both move to the city because of a job opportunity.

Patrilocality is ambiguous in other ways, too. Hiba emphasized that like her mother before her, she had to separate from her family of descent when she married, even though her parents lived in a neighboring village. However, after having been her friend over a prolonged period, I observed that her mother was physically present in her life in significant ways, such as being present at both her births and for other family events. And then, while daughters emphasized the loss they felt at marriage and even more so around birth, the stories also weaved a continuity between generations and strengthened relationships between daughters and mothers. Indeed, with longitudinal work, I noticed the importance of maternal families in growing families. This reminded me that in the business of collecting stories, anthropologists must remember that stories are never finished. Building on Aristotle, MacIntyre (1981) writes in his work on the human as a "storytelling animal" that human beings are characters in enacted narratives and that "like characters in a fictional narrative we do not know what will happen next, but none the less, our lives have a certain form which projects itself towards our future" (216). He insists on the unpredictability

19. Based on her fieldwork in the Galilee, Lilian Abou-Tabickh (2010, 2012) refers to women's migration to their husband's village or town as an "invisible migration" that is not recognized as migration. Instead, it is internalized as a natural part of the life course. Her interlocutors who migrate to their husbands' family town tell her they continue to be considered *gharība* (foreign), even after years of living in the new locality.

of people's lives as well as their teleological nature. Humans don't know what will happen later in their lives; however, they still hope and make decisions in the present as if they can discern what will happen in the future. Humans live out a story that runs from birth and is not finished until death. Thus, by definition, stories are unfinished until death.

Conclusion

In following and narrating the birth stories of Rama and Hiba, I was surprised to hear stories about loss and loneliness. The anthropology of birth on the one hand focuses on medicalization. On the other hand, the social science literature on loneliness focuses on connections to industrialization, capitalism, and urbanization. There are experiences common to many around the world with displacement, exile, and closed borders affecting huge parts of the world population that cannot be captured either by medicalization or by thinking about loneliness in terms of industrial societies. The analyses of the narratives of loss and loneliness shed light on these experiences.

Palestine studies would probably look skeptically on an analysis based on the concepts of loneliness and loss because they sound depoliticized. And in this analysis, I refrain from using the frame of the oppositional practices of everyday life. Yet, I argue nevertheless that the political imaginary shapes experiences of loss and loneliness. Lori Allen's concept of "getting by" describes the kinds of subjects that occupation constructs; I ask how a subjectivity of "getting by" affects intimate relationships. I show that it produces loss and loneliness. This is particularly true in the Middle East because of patriarchal connectivity, with birth being a moment when patriarchal connective relationships are particularly visible. The loneliness is connected to patrilocality, too. But patrilocality is complicated, first, because not all newlyweds move to the husband's community, but also because with longitudinal work, I notice connections to mothers and families of origin that remain important parts of new mothers' lives, despite the deep sense of loneliness they feel at birth.

2

Midwives' Oral Histories of Struggle

During my work in hospital labor rooms, I became friends with nurse-midwives who taught me about birth and how to assist in them as well as about the cities where they worked and their villages and camps of origin. In the middle of my fieldwork year, in March 2004, one midwife invited me to her dorm room after her shift and said that if I wanted to know about birth, I needed to collect their oral histories (*tārīkh shafawi*). She was a refugee from a camp near Bethlehem and a particularly politicized and intellectual midwife who read the newest Arabic novels and followed the political maneuverings of personalities in the Palestinian Authority. Most midwives and many new mothers I met, when asked about child-birth and the work assisting it, responded with a life-history type of narra-tive. Starting with their village of origin, parents, childhood, and studies, they described stages of the life cycle punctuated by political events. The nurse-midwives' oral histories had a common and consistent narrative arc, beginning with a life of poverty, a middle about struggle, and ending with an uncertain future. They focused their narratives on themselves as independent, working, struggling, and gendered persons and referred to specific events, dates, and places, including information about economic and social processes, such as income, profession, and labor.

Anthropologists have long used oral histories as data. For example, students of Franz Boas first used the oral history method to document the lives of Native North Americans (Radin 1926). Scholars considered the life history a documentary device to represent the characteristic for-mative experiences of persons in a particular culture through the case of a specific individual. In the 1920s and 1930s, scholars from the Chicago School of Sociology conducted oral history to document the lives of criminals, prostitutes, and other marginalized groups in urban centers in an effort to provide social solutions to their problems. In the 1960s and 1970s, the oral history method grew with the influence of feminist and anti-colonial movements. In 1961 Jan Vansina published *Oral Tradition as History*, in which he promoted the use of interdisciplinary tools to recover African history.

During the 1980s, anthropologists began to experiment with the method by bringing to light the relationships between anthropologists and their informants to reveal how a life history is jointly constructed (Crapanzano 1980; Shostak 1980). Vincent Crapanzano (1980) presents the life history and his elicitation of the interview as a puzzle for which he asks the reader's help to interpret. Crapanzano's interlocutor, Tuhami, would convey a sense of his pain by grasping for vivid metaphors, whether they came from what we recognize as real life or from fantasy. Crapanzano argues that the psychic processes and linguistic metaphors of fantasy are a valid means of communicating experience. However, they require considerably greater skill in interpretation than more realist modes of narration.

Rosemary Sayigh (1998) found that younger Palestinian women in Lebanon structured their oral histories around national historical landmarks and included their political and public activities in the foreground. Their life histories are replete with political events, dates, places, and progress in a chronological format she attributes to the increasing importance of state institutions and national politics during the time of the revolution among Palestinian refugees in Lebanon.[1]

1. Beginning with "Black September" 1970, King Hussein's troops expelled the Palestine Liberation Organization, led by Yasser Arafat, from Jordan. Many fighters, along with their families, fled to Lebanon over the year that followed. The "Revolution" (i.e., the PLO leadership) then settled in Beirut, with the headquarters in a West Beirut neighborhood. Until its expulsion by Israel in 1982 and subsequent reestablishment in Tunis, the PLO and its Lebanese allies found itself in virtual control of much of the territory from Beirut south to the Israeli border. During the early phases of the Lebanese Civil War (1975–90), the PLO found itself drawn in on the "Muslim-Progressive" side. By 1976, that

In Hayden White's pioneering study (1973), he traces the major changes in nineteenth-century European history and social theory registered at the level of techniques for writing about society. He argues that any work of history or social theory exhibits emplotment, argument, and ideological implications.[2] These may be in an unstable relation to the facts they attempt to write about and order. These instabilities show connections to the social world and the historical moment. For White, romance is the empathetic self-identification by the writer with quests that transcend specific periods of world history (8). It is a drama symbolized by the hero's transcendence of the world of experience and by the transcendence of good over evil (9). White gives the example of the historian of the French Revolution Jules Michelet, who plotted his histories as dramas of disclosure of the liberation of a spiritual power fighting to free itself from the forces of darkness, a redemption (152). For Michelet, White writes, the task of the historian is to serve as a preserver of what is redeemed, a "resurrection" (152). His romantic emplotment of the history of France up to the revolution was set within the larger tragic awareness of its subsequent dissipation. But the tragedy is set as a phase in the total process, to be annulled in the fire of the revolution which his own histories were meant to keep alive.

The narrative arc and plot of the life histories of midwives in my work resemble White's characterization of romance, but ethnographic attention in the context of the Palestinian Occupied Territories also revealed disjunctive stories that broke with the romantic narrative structure fixed by precise time-place chronology. For example, Tahrir's narrative, which I relate in detail below, is structured by precise dates, times, and chronological events, but as she tells her divorce story, that common chronological

---

side being on the cusp of a smashing victory against the "Christian" camp, Syria intervened to save it, becoming Arafat's major adversary, and consolidating its own control of the country over the next thirty years.

2. Hayden White coined the term *emplotment* to highlight the idea that stories are made. They are not simply found in historical data. Historical meaning is imposed on historical facts by means of a choice of plot type, and this choice is inevitably ethical and political.

structure becomes messy. For instance, I could no longer tell how long she had been living without her children or for how many years her ex-husband had kept them from her. I heard her saying that she was worried she would not be able to teach her children the ability to withstand struggle, which was a central characteristic of the rest of her oral history. Disruptions to the structure of oral histories appear in other ways, too. Some midwives intersperse their chronological oral histories with language from an older generation of rural and refugee communities. For example, Suhaila presents a clear and chronological oral history with a narrative arc typical of midwives, but at a certain point in the narrative, she intersperses her stories with contrasting speech that does not flow and which sounds poetic, rather than narrative. While anthropologists could choose to ignore the short disjunctive moments in the oral histories and present a flowing chronological narrative, bringing these moments to light points to important conditions of the midwives' lives.

In this chapter, I explore the oral histories of Tahrir and Suhaila, which I recorded in their dorm rooms. I knew them both well. They worked in one of the hospitals where I was doing fieldwork and we became friends. They narrated their unique stories, characteristic of the genre of oral histories: clear, consistent, and typical in terms of plot and tone. They referred to places, dates, and political events, but in certain moments of the recording, ruptures in the clear narrative occurred. For Tahrir, dates, time, and stories became jumbled when she spoke of her divorce. She viewed herself as a strong and struggling person and as capable of transmitting that strength to her children. However, her years of separation from her children made her question her sense of self and, at the time of the recording, it was still uncertain how often she would get to see her children and, thus, how much she could influence them.

While Suhaila did not face a deep sense of crisis like Tahrir's separation from her children, her narrative too had moments of disjuncture and shifts into what sounded like jumbled speech or epic poetry, "Ottomans killed rebellious hearts," she said at one point in her chronological and clear narrative. Folklorists Ibrahim Muhawi and Sharif Kanaana (1989, 2), identify two types of storytelling in Palestinian society: the fable (ḥikāya) and the story (qiṣa). While the ḥikāya is fiction and involves fantasy, the *qiṣa* appears more realistic, describing historical events that could have happened, such as the epic story of Abu Zeid Al-Hilali or tales of Bedouin raids and adventure. The *qiṣa* uses poetry and narrates the deeds and adventures of heroic figures of the past. I heard Suhaila's interjection at the end of a realist anecdote, recognizing it as a sentence borrowed from the *qiṣa* genre, as she got confused telling family stories of political violence.

In Norbert Elias's *The Civilizing Mission* (1994 [1939]), he writes about the ways in which language and manners changed over the course of the sixteenth through the eighteenth centuries in Western Europe, as bourgeois people strove to adopt court language and manners. Behaviors like blowing your nose with your hands and using vulgar words became no longer acceptable. Schools, private lessons, and etiquette books contributed to transforming manners and language among the bourgeoisie. However, popular language and manners persisted for a longer time among the lower and marginalized classes. In the Arab world, oral stories and epic poetry, which I discuss below, are most vibrant in rural and underserved areas. I interpret Suhaila's momentary departures into poetic language as reflective of her rural and remote upbringing. Like many midwives, she was the first generation in her family and community to go to school, let alone university. Thus, her narrative wavered between a consistent and realist oral history narrative and momentary opaque and poetic sentences.

These are two different life stories. Tahrir is an urban refugee and a divorced woman from the Bethlehem area. From an early age, her family pushed her and her sibling to get an education. Suhaila is an unmarried midwife from the rural Tulkarem area. Unlike the cliché about Palestinian families, hers did not focus on education, instead directing children toward crafts that do not require years of study. Both histories pay attention to the relationship of their family to agricultural land and emphasize being independent, working, and gendered persons. Both follow the common narrative arc of the oral histories I found in most histories I collected. They began with a life of poverty, continued with a middle of struggle through studies, managing families and work, and finished with an uncertain future. But at specific moments in the narrative, they depart from the consistent structure of clear dates, places, and political events.

Tahrir's Story

After her shift, Tahrir and I went to her room in the nurses' dorms that she shared with a colleague who was out. She made us tea and we sat on her bed. She started by saying that if she had to talk about birth, I should record her *tārīkh shafawi* (oral history) and she would tell me about her family and her work. I said, "Well, let me turn the recorder on. Where shall we start?" Like many of the oral history interviews I conducted, I started with this question. During the rest of my recording, my questions were few and mostly requests for clarification.

"We are originally from Saidiyya," she said as I turned on the recorder for the first time. "It is in between Jerusalem and the coast . . . I visited when I was little. After that, until I was about twenty, I did not visit it because the situation became worse . . . My parents fled [in 1948] and moved to Aisha camp." Tahrir, born in 1966, does not remember the wars of 1948 and 1967. Unlike her parents, she knows only life between her camp, near Bethlehem, and Jerusalem, where she has always worked. Her narrative, thus, begins prior to her birth, with her village of origin and 1948, an approach typical of younger refugees. These beginnings, as Edward Said (1975) noted in relation to modern texts, are a first step in the intentional production of meaning. Tahrir both activates and limits what is permitted in the oral history by mobilizing the loss of her village and land and, crucially, the loss of a subsistence agricultural base.

After their expulsion, her father found work on a construction site in Israel, the lowest paid job after an agricultural laborer, lower than iron-workers and carpenters. Her mother was a homemaker. They were both illiterate. Her father had been to school until the second grade and her mother never set foot in a school. Tahrir and her six sisters and two brothers went to schools operated by the United Nations Relief and Works Agency for Palestinian Refugees (UNRWA).[3] To supplement their income,

---

3. The United Nations Relief and Works Agency for Palestinian Refugees (UNRWA) was established in the wake of the 1948 exodus, to care for refugees. It offers educational and health services as well as support in the areas of infrastructure and relief.

on Fridays and during summer vacation, the children worked in an Israeli linen factory.[4] The schools were free and most of the nine children did well academically. The eldest sister studied nursing for two years, then immediately started working and supported their household. Tahrir proudly explained how she and her sisters, one after the other, worked and paid for their siblings' education, which is consistent with Maya Rosenfeld's mapping of "familial work chains" (Rosenfeld 2002, 521), where unmarried, educated, and professionally employed women spent their salary supporting and educating their siblings.

Tahrir's oral history was a typical one for her generation. It began with her village of origin, from which her family was expelled, and is structured by watershed dates in contemporary history. The year 1948 is particularly prominent, as well as 1967, 1987, and 2000, as well as other regional political events, such as the 1980s "war of the camps" in Lebanon and "Black September" in Jordan.[5] In addition, the oral history indicates precise places, such as the official name and geographical location of her village. Few would know its location, as it has been destroyed, her refugee camp,

4. Hiring Palestinian children and women in Israeli factories and agriculture was common in the 1970s and 1980s. The place where Israeli employers picked up child employees to work was known as "the market of children" in Israeli public culture of the time (Zamir 1979).

5. The PLO, founded in 1964, was at first considered a useful tool of the major Arab countries. Until the defeat of June 1967 at the hands of Israel, Jordan saw little reason to curtail the organization's recruitment campaigns, centered in the refugee camps. This changed progressively, beginning with the highly symbolic battle of Karameh in 1968, in which irregular PLO forces led by Yasser Arafat, supported by Jordanian artillery, repulsed the Israeli attack on the Karameh military base. Buoyed by this feat, thousands of young people flocked to one or another of the PLO factions, mainly Arafat's Fatah group, enlisting as *fidayīn* (guerrilla fighters) in the cause of freedom and self-determination. From that moment on, the Palestinian presence in Jordan became an existential threat for King Hussein and the Jordanian establishment. Indeed, the PLO was tempted to seek power, Palestinians being in the numerical majority in Jordan. King Hussein finally responded with a concerted military campaign, beginning in September 1970 and lasting until the following summer, through which PLO members, armed and administrative, were driven out of the country. Most of them regrouped in Lebanon.

as well as nearby streets and neighborhoods in Jerusalem. Furthermore, oral histories refer to precise sociological information regarding professions, number of family members per household, household income, and housing situation. Finally, oral histories with a younger generation indicate institutions such as specific schools, hospitals, prisons, and political parties. Thus, the narrative is clear, specific, and chronological in ways that give it a realist, sociological, and modern tone.

As children, Tahrir continued, they thought they lived comfortably. But when her sister started working and her family started to rely on her sister's salary, she became conscious of just how poor her family was.

Throughout her narrative, Tahrir discusses wage labor and its pay, benefits, location, and prestige. At every phase of her life, Tahrir describes the ways her family survived, sometimes with details such as work location, prestige of the work, salary amount, and the number of working hours. Regarding her childhood, she says,

> We worked as children on Fridays and school vacations in an Israeli clothing company to cover the house's needs because honestly we were very poor. Our situation was bad, really bad . . . My father was a laborer . . . he had seven girls and two boys, all in school. How would he be able to cover the needs of the house? He had the lowest paying job, not an ironworker, not a carpenter, a laborer . . . So, we worked whenever we could without leaving school. And my sister, she finished her diploma, started working [as a nurse] and started spending her money on us . . .

Tahrir connects wage work to her suffering, not just because she and her father before her worked tiring jobs, but because Zionist land acquisition through purchase or expropriation before and after the establishment of the state of Israel is associated with the displacement of peasants, creating more Palestinian wage labor. The proletarianization of Palestinian peasants started during the British Mandate period when villagers took day jobs as workers in Arab and British businesses, such as citrus orchards and railway construction. But the population remained rural (Laurens 2002), as is the case of her father, who continued to cultivate a small plot of agricultural land. It was not until the mass expropriation of land after 1948, and then again after 1967, that considerable urbanization took place, as refugees regrouped in towns and urbanized camps. After 1967 the Israeli labor market opened to Palestinians in the Occupied Territories, and most families like Tahrir's had at least one person employed as a laborer in Israel.

Creating jobs in Palestinian institutions and businesses instead of relying on the Israeli market was a key measure promoted by the Palestine Liberation Organization (PLO) in exile to support the population of the Occupied Territories, while promoting itself as a national entity (Sayigh 1997, 479–82). The PLO called such measures *sumud* (steadfastness) policy, a set of economic policies for reshaping cultural expression and experience. Rhetorically, it made "just staying put in Palestine" a political stance. You did not need to join political parties or the resistance movement, you just needed to remain on the land of Palestine and refrain from emigrating. The PLO gave people the means to do so by infusing capital into institutions and businesses, and thus creating jobs. According to the ideology of the time, lasting solutions to material problems could only be achieved through liberation since poverty was a function of colonial rule. The sumud policy was thus a transient socioeconomic approach, a measure to keep things going until liberation was achieved. The policy is difficult to document because the PLO was an outlawed organization in Israel and the Occupied Territories. Receiving funds from the PLO was against the law and therefore never acknowledged officially. However, Israel turned a blind eye to the PLO infusing funds into the Occupied Territories and it became a well-known secret that all sorts of institutions received PLO money, from the prestigious hospital in Jerusalem to the little ice cream parlor in Ramallah.

Sumud appeared in popular culture too. The prototypical image of sumud was that of an old man, with a back curved by the erosion of time, tending to his gigantic, deeply rooted olive tree. There are many famous and widely circulated versions of these kinds of images in Palestinian poster art from the 1980s.[6] Before the 1970s, sumud was present as

---

6. See in particular the artwork printed on postcards and posters of Sliman Masour (b. 1947) and Nabil Anani (b. 1943). It was common for people to put up these posters

a concept among Palestinians in the Galilee, for example, but it was not a political program championed by a political organization. In 1964 Mahmoud Darwish's poem (1993 [1964]), "On Perseverance," ('an aṣumūd) invokes agriculture and land against military rule. It ends with "the earth, the farmer and persistence, tell me, how can they be defeated? These three substances, how can they be defeated?" (Darwish 1993 [1964], my translation). The Palestinian resistance movement, upon its emergence in the mid-1960s, deployed symbols from rural culture (Swedenburg 2003), for example, the ḥaṭa (headscarf, which Yasser Arafat wore), dabka (a folkloric dance of the greater Syrian region), and taṭrīz (a type of embroidery).[7] Many nationalist songs were variations on the repertoire of traditional music, replete with images of the olive tree, the prickly pear, and harvest. Tahrir's oral history continually showed her attachment to land and peasantry. On some of my visits to her parents' house in the refugee camp or to the house she moved to in the outskirts of Bethlehem years later, she took me walking with her son on lands that had belonged to her village of origin before 1948. Tahrir connected herself to her village history by invoking food, song, and language and by narrating the process of being evicted from the village, thus losing their livelihood and depending on low-paid wage labor.

Despite her illiteracy, Tahrir's mother insisted on her children studying. During the end of high school exams, she would stay with them as they studied and support them. In Tahrir's oral history, her mother had paved the way for children to work by showing them (zara'at fina, literally

---

or postcards in their homes. Motherhood is also often represented as a figure of sumud. Nabil Anani, one of Palestine's leading contemporary artists (b. 1943) painted a famous painting titled *Motherhood* (1979). The phenomenon is explained in numerous critical works such as Bardenstein (1997).

7. This celebration of rural culture contrasts with the dominant culture of schools in Palestine during the first half of the twentieth century. Lisa Taraki (2013) documents how writers of memoirs from Ramallah and neighboring villages, such as Omar Salih al-Barghouti and Jiryes Mansour, explained how the Jerusalem and Ramallah schools taught them to despise rural culture and praise urban culture, even teaching them how to speak a Jerusalem dialect instead of a Ramallah or other village dialect.

"planted in us") the value of education. "She insisted that we study . . . She refused that we, the girls, marry young. She turned down suitors one after the other when we were fourteen, fifteen, sixteen, seventeen. Education was very important. For us, the girls, this is what she engrained in us." This insistence on the importance of education is echoed in many Palestinian refugee communities with cliché sentences such as "All we have left is education," or as Tahrir said her mother told her, "Education is your only way out of the camp."

In Tahrir's narrative, the pressure to get an education and the obligation to work is gendered. Male family members often spent years in jail or sacrificed their school performance for time-consuming work as organizers in political parties. Furthermore, the closure made it easier for women than men to acquire permits or cross borders. Rising through the ranks of the educational system was a way to secure a decent income for the family, but it also provided women financial independence which, in some cases, was a way out of a troubled marriage. Tahrir recognized that work both tied her down to an exhausting lifestyle and gave her "independence." She attributed the possibility of divorce in her own life, and in the lives of other women of her generation (but not her mother's), to employment. She never questioned her expenses for educating her siblings (which she and her sisters gradually contributed to as they started working), but she resented her husband's control over her salary.

In her story, the women fared better than men economically and socially. While all the girls and one of the boys studied and became financially independent, Tahrir felt that her second brother did not learn how to persevere. He never liked school, to his mother's disappointment, and instead finished a technical degree. He worked in a restaurant in Israel and "never tried to get somewhere." Then, the Israeli army made it illegal for anyone to go into Israel without a permit. He got a false ID and permits from a friend and worked in the same restaurant. Then the Israeli authorities caught him and imprisoned him for two years. Now he had no money and no job. "In the end, he lost a lot of things." Her brother's story is like her husband's. She, in vain, urged him to "study or do something and face reality," but her brother and husband succumbed to the same forces she and her other siblings had learned to surmount.

Like many of her colleagues, Tahrir lived in perpetual exhaustion. She changed jobs, moving from a charitable hospital, where she had worked since graduation, to a small private-sector clinic because it was closer to home. However, she discovered longer working hours at the whim of the establishment, which further destabilized her marriage. She stopped working completely and stayed at home for six months, hoping it might push her husband to find a job. Instead, they fell into debt, and so Tahrir returned to her job in Jerusalem. She had been unable to rid herself of the need to work for wages. The long commutes involving curfews and waiting at checkpoints, and her husband's resentment of her work and absence, were exhausting.

On most days, Tahrir waited at checkpoints to get to work and/or to get home. The state of the waiting person is one of agitation and striving to get somewhere. Waiting, Vincent Crapanzano (1985) emphasized, is being locked in a present that is always subordinated to a contingent future.[8] Such is the case of many Palestinian people. It is impossible to know until the very last minute whether a necessary permit is granted, how long it will take to pass through a particular checkpoint, or even if any will open. In response, people have found myriad ways to get through the closure system, including taking back roads, walking across hills, climbing walls, and producing fake permits. Many people manage laboriously to twist themselves into the nexus of fragmented political, economic, and family life in Palestine today. Still others, failing to find strategies and alliances to make their lives habitable and purposeful, lose the energy needed to persist in what is commonly called "the big prison."[9]

Tahrir was only thirty-eight years old, but I could see the tiredness on her wrinkled face and hands. Tahrir's female colleagues referred to her as "stubborn" and as having "a difficult life" because she did not find stability in her marriage. A wool blanket covered the bed in the room provided by the hospital where Tahrir sat, her veil and coat still on. With a life

8. For other works on waiting, see Hage (2009); Jamal (2016); Peteet (2018); Salih (2018); and Wick (2006, 2011).
9. "The big prison" is the metaphor that many people use to talk about living with restrictions on mobility, living under occupation and the closure.

divided between this room and her parents' house, she had few belongings, a teapot, biscuits, a Qur'an, and two books. She told me she dealt
with constant *ta'ab nafsī* (emotional exhaustion) due to a sense of fatigue
coming from her "never giving up" in the face of economic, political, and
domestic strife. Tahrir was exhausted by her work as a nurse-midwife,
her commute, her three difficult children, and her ongoing problems with
her ex-husband. Her exhaustion stemmed from a suffering accumulated
over her lifetime. Caroline Bledsoe's (2002) analysis of demographic and
survey information in rural Gambia unveils how her interlocutors understood ageing as a process of accumulation and becoming old as a process
of becoming "worn out" rather than the passage of chronological time.
In this vision, an old person is wrinkled, has sagging flesh, and flaccid
muscles and painful joints. Neither chronological age nor attaining meno-
pause speed up ageing. Rather, it is the contingencies of life, such as sick-
ness, hunger, strenuous work, and especially reproductive events, such as
repeated births, that mark a woman's age.

Tahrir's understanding of exhaustion resonates with Bledsoe's notion
of accumulation. Indeed, she thought of herself as being so exhausted as
a result of the various forms of violence that accumulated in her life. Tahrir married in the camp at age twenty-two as she took up her job at the
hospital. But her marriage was problematic from the start. For example,
she started a BA program alongside her job, but her husband made her
drop out. And they tried for three years but failed to get pregnant. Their
difficulty having children was due to events that happened when she was
sixteen. In 1982, following an attempt by the Israeli army to close off the
camp by encircling it with a wall and putting checkpoints at all entrances,
she took part in a demonstration where she was injured by a bullet in her
stomach. The night of the demonstration, her parents were asleep when
Tahrir slipped out of the house with one of her sisters. She was rushed to
the governmental hospital in Hebron, where they operated to stitch up her
stomach. Her stay at the hospital was a turning point for her. She met and
observed nurses. Their work made them closer to what it is to be human,
she thought, and from that point she worked and planned to become one
herself. The injury had bodily and social consequences, causing three years
of injury-related infertility. Finally, her doctor prescribed hormones, which

led to her giving birth to twins, who she described as loud and crazy. She worked at night because she could not be away from home during the day and went straight home after work.

A year after the birth of her twins, she enrolled in a midwifery program in defiance of her husband. For a year and a half, she coped with babies, work, and training. Then, she gave birth to another baby. With three small children, she continued working and studying. Tahrir held a tenacious grip on her activities, which aggravated her marital relationship, generating yet another form of violence in her everyday life. Working the night shift, she spent more time away from home. Sometimes she worked several shifts back-to-back so she could return to her camp in Bethlehem and stay with her children for a full day, a situation that irritated her husband, who had no work. She described him as uneducated and having fallen prey to the conditions of his life. A political activist in Fatah, he was not allowed to enter Israel even before the closure became generalized. He wanted to live the bourgeois gender practices, whereby he worked and earned a living for his family and his wife stayed home. But the intersection of Israeli restrictions on movement and his lack of education made this impossible. Tahrir earned, 2000 Israeli shekels a month (approximately $600). For a short period of time, when her husband was employed by the Palestinian Ministry of Health, he made 1,200 shekels. But more often than not, he was unemployed. There was a time period during the Gulf War when Jerusalem was completely closed off; the nurses stayed on site for a week and returned home for a day. This created problems in her marriage, but they could not live without her income. During that time period, "there was absolutely no work for anybody apart from us in the hospitals." She would go home for a day and find her husband sitting at home or playing cards. "He had such emptiness," she said. "But these are the conditions of our life. And I have a conviction that these conditions can be changed or ameliorated."

Tahrir's narration of the early years of her marriage shows how oral histories often weave political events, labor, health of the body, and legacy for children. Her bullet injury hurt her body and her marriage; her second birth occurred during the generalized siege, following the Hebron massacre of Palestinians by a settler; her wage work aggravated the marital problems; and the gendered closure and labor market angered her husband, thus producing another form of violence. As her married life continued, it became another site where Tahrir had to persevere. For ten years, she lived with him, although she spent more time at her parents' house than in their conjugal home. "Every year, it was a must that he kick me out for a month or two." He would then send people over to her parent's house to ask her to return. She got so tired of being hit and listening to "go to your father's house." Finally, she told him, "This time I will not leave." She stayed until the next day, when he went out, and she prepared a bag with her belongings. She took her books, her ID card, and her clothes, and never returned to their conjugal home. Her husband sent many people to seek reconciliation, but she had had enough.

She then lived with her parents for six years, but her husband would not agree to a divorce. She gained custody of her children through the courts by way of laws that accord the mother custody if the children are young and she does not remarry. She took them to her parents' house, where they stayed until their father started taking them from her. For example, he would collect them from school and not return them home, or the children would go outside to play, and he would take them. They all lived in the same camp and so he bumped into them sometimes. Once, she was taking her son to work with her because he had a fever and they bumped into her husband. They started fighting and shouting at each other, and people passing by came over to see if they could help. She found herself going to the Palestinian police every day, trying to get her children back from him. When enough pressure was placed on him, her husband would send the children back, but after a day or two, he would take them again.

All this affected the children: "They went crazy," (*ṣar 'indhum halwasa*). They were afraid that their father would take them and eventually stopped wanting to go to school. When their father picked them up, they would start crying and yelling. It was distressing for her and created problems for her parents because her husband would fight and insult them in their neighborhood. The children would refuse to go with him, but then the police would get involved, and everyone just wanted the drama to end, but the children felt forced to go to their father's place. Much of this occurred while Tahrir was working.

From the bits and pieces I stitched together, it seems that for a period of six months, she did not see her twins. Only the youngest was with her. She went to the courts again, demanding visitation rights to her twins. But when the children started seeing her, they wanted to come back and live with her, which was impossible and so caused sorrow. She got so tired of the back and forth and the whole separation story. The police were also tired of the story and did very little to help her. They would go to his house, but her husband would not give them the children. There are multiple reasons the police do little to help Tahrir in this story, despite her legal standing. To start with, families and offspring belong first and foremost to the father (Joseph 2000). This value is visible in multiple aspects of the personal status law in the West Bank. Fathers retain guardianship of children, making them responsible for important decisions such as education and marriage. Usually, mothers are given physical custody (ḥaḍāna) of boys until the age of nine and girls until the age of eleven, and fathers thereafter (Welchman 2000). Thus, not taking the children away from their father was the path of least resistance for the police. In addition, the police and Palestinian Authority have little executive power. They have recourse to jail only in exceptional cases. Their mode of work is usually convincing and threatening. Tahrir's husband managed to tire the police and wear her down to the point that she dropped the charges against him but obtained her divorce in return.

After the police gave up on her husband, she did not see her children in the open for another two years. She saw them secretly at school, or relatives would arrange for secret meetings in their homes. She would follow them clandestinely as they went back and forth from school or to the store. Sometimes, she did not even plan it but would find herself in their path. She cried as she told this part of her story, her guilt and grief palpable. Unlike the rest of her oral history, which was clear, chronological, and referred to dates of political events, this part confused dates and times and lacked the previous clarity. I never understood how much time she was separated from her children or how she was able to get them back years later. This part of the story is opaque. It did not adhere to the structure of dates, times, and events. These concepts were of little importance. In fact, they were supplanted by the emotionality of the narrative that focused on her suffering and how she felt at the time of the separation and at the time of narration.

She believed her husband was punishing her because she had sued, and the courts fined him for not paying alimony. She repeated that she did not want the money but instead used it and the courts as pressure to see her children. In a first agreement, she was awarded alimony from the courts, which she used for her children. In the end, she got a divorce, but at a steep cost. She repeated that she wanted nothing but the children and that he knew she would not let go of the children in court. She would have remained married to him her whole life if the condition of the divorce was not seeing the children. The divorce agreement in court awarded her weekly visitation with her children and that the youngest live with her. For the first week it worked, but then her husband broke the agreement and took the child from her and she stopped seeing the youngest too. So, she retracted all her demands for financial support and compensation. She considers that over the years of her married life, her husband took the money she deposited in a joint account and put it in a savings account under his name, supposedly to save to build a house. This proved to be true because after their divorce, he found money to buy a Mercedes (to work as a taxi driver) and remarry, both of which are expensive endeavors. Now, she sometimes thinks that she acted too quickly by giving up her demands. But she was so tired, she was willing to concede to anything just to get some rest. And, she was worried about the negative effects of the divorce on her children. All three children suffered from nightmares.

She finally decided to stop fighting with their father but, as a result, experienced the hardest time of her life. She was tired, afraid, felt guilty, and was crying all the time. She escaped reality by sleeping: "I would sleep all the time after I got back from work. I did not want to wake up. And then I started hearing voices. I would hear my children's voices all the time. I would imagine one of them calling for me." She would see a mother and child in the street and collapse. She saw her children's nightmares and fears as an extension of her own, and the idea that she was not transmitting the strength to wait and struggle in everyday life possessed her. With time, she said she got used to her children not being with her. She busied herself with studies at the university and with work and daily prayers.

Her studies distracted her thoughts from her children. Had she not gone back to studying, she would have gotten worse. The importance of sumud (perseverance) appears in the pathos of Tahrir's separation from her children and her feared inability to transfer sumud to them. She wanted to be with her children because by seeing her struggle everyday they would learn how to struggle. They must see their mother as strong, striving every day to work, getting permits, and working at home. Indeed, it is because she refused to seem weak in front of her children that she divorced. She didn't want them to grow up seeing their mother abused and insulted. She lost years of being with her children, but in the end, she hoped that during her short weekend visits with her children, she could transmit to them her strength to struggle every day. Her ongoing crisis and uncertainty were due to her separation from her children and that she could not show them perseverance and motherly care.

Like many oral histories of midwives of her generation, Tahrir's oral history began with a story of childhood poverty. Then, it became a story of work, struggle, and suffering in her young adult life. The oral story is structured by precise dates and places as well as chronological events. In particular, she references watershed dates in the recent history of Palestine, 1948, 1967, 1987, and 2000, and situates herself within that communal history. The narrative presents sociological information about place, age, origin, work, profession, income, and household. The ending of her oral history is uncertain. This too is typical of midwives' oral histories. At the time of the oral history, they are still in the midst of their work and careers and building their households. Yet, in this chronological and sociological narrative, one part is opaque, the discussion of her separation from her children. It is not clear how long she was separated from them or what happened during what may have been years. In the end, what is most striking is the strong sense of the gendered, independent self that emerges in the oral history.

I continued seeing Tahrir regularly after the oral history interview and followed her story for years. Tahrir's living arrangement had changed when I visited her in her home again in 2014. She had moved out of her parents' home and had rented an apartment on the outskirts of the camp (which signifies upward mobility), and her children lived with her. Two were in university and the youngest in secondary school. Her husband had a new family and no longer tormented them (although she said he remained important for legal decisions, such as her children's marriage). She provided everything for her children, and I could feel the warmth and stability in their relationships. It seemed that sumud had paid off. She gave me a bag of fresh thyme that she and her youngest had picked on the lands of her village of origin and requested that I make zaatar pastries for my children when I got to Beirut.

Suhaila's Story

Suhaila's life experiences were different from Tahrir's, but the plot and narrative tropes of the oral history were similar and typical of midwives' oral histories. She used romance to tell her story, with quests to document her life of struggle to live better lives. She referred to her village of origin, the members of her household, her housing situation, marriage, age, and her family members' education, profession, and income. Suhaila's background was different from Tahrir's, however. While Tahrir had a distinctly urban upbringing, Suhaila grew up in a remote village in the northern West Bank. Suhaila moved to cities in her adult life, first to Jericho, then Ramallah, then Jerusalem. Suhaila's deep rural upbringing meant she was exposed and probably fluent in multiple forms of storytelling. As I will discuss in the next chapter, oral history is a contemporary form of storytelling practiced by younger generations of both rural and urban people. But *qiṣaṣ* and epic poetry are a distinctly rural type of storytelling practiced by an older generation. Suhaila performed the oral history narrative well and told a sociological and realistic story. But at times, it was interspersed with sentences from an older and rural type of storytelling, sentences from epic poetry or stories of heroes and adventures that lacked the references to time and space that the rest of her narrative contained.

Suhaila was born in Tulkarem in 1976. Her parents had nine children, four girls and five boys. Her father was a construction worker in Israel and owned the house she and her siblings grew up in. Neither he nor her mother were educated (*mish muta'allimīn*). She was reproachful of her parents for not encouraging their children to study:

My father should have encouraged us to study. But what happened was the opposite. He would say things like "Where am I going to find the money to educate you? I don't have money." But as you know, if the eldest son or daughter studies, he educates all his siblings. So, we were a bit confused. What are we going to do? Are we going to study, get married, work? How are we going to build a future for ourselves? . . . A long time ago, the university fees were relatively cheap. One semester was eighty dinars. Today, the semester costs about four hundred dinars. My father did not have that urge to educate his children. To take away a bit of money from food and drink and put into educating his first child, for example. The idea of education is not very central to my father's life. I am not singling out my father; I am talking about my community. To educate your children you have to have that idea that you will push for education. Of course, economic conditions play a role, but at that time, when the university fees were cheap, it would have been possible to study. My father could have sent my eldest brother to university and then he would have educated the second. The story is about a sort of ignorance.

Thus, she considers herself from a rural class that does not value education. Very early on in her narrative, I recognized the sociological and realistic story she was crafting.

Suhaila's four elder siblings finished the exam at the end of high school and started working. One brother dropped out of school earlier. Her brothers and sisters married and had children. And now she thinks their economic situation is good. They built lives for themselves, built a house, got married, had children. One of her younger brothers studied archeology and tourism at Najah University, but he never found work in the field. There are no job opportunities and the few opportunities that do exist, she said, worked through connections, wasṭa. So he worked in construction in Israel, married, and has a daughter. He is the only sibling with a BA.

She thinks most of her siblings' limited education is about their class situation and an environment that encouraged young people to become adults through other institutions, such as crafts (ṣanʿa). Her brothers finished the exam at the end of high school, and then worked in Israel in construction. At the same time, they each learned a craft. "They constructed their futures through their crafts. One works in the field of electricity, the other in the field of tiles and the third is an employee of the Palestinian Authority. In addition, each has founded a home, spends on his family, and their situation is ok." They each managed to build sustainable lives for themselves. As for the sisters, one studied *sharī'a* law for two years and got a diploma. Her two eldest sisters finished the exam at the end of high school and got married. She returned to the history of learning and education multiple times during her interview:

> My grandfather was not educated, nor were my aunts. My extended family on both the maternal and paternal sides of the family are not educated. We do not have that kind of emphasis on learning. Of course, had our parents educated us, we would have been better off. However, what can we do? They used to work the land. Their source of income was from the land. They spent on their houses from the work on the land . . . Then, one day, my father started working in construction in Israel.

Thus, Suhaila does not consider herself and her family as poor, but as people who a generation ago were comfortable living off the land. In her life story as in many others, the shift to wage labor in Israel is a turning point in the family history. Nevertheless, she explained that her family continued to live off the land. All her family, to this day, rely on their land to live, in addition to wage labor. However, it is no longer the most important part of their income. "The work of the land is part of our lives, but," she said, "it is unreliable, you always fear the atmospheric conditions. You get rain or you do not get rain. It is tiring and you do not make enough money from it. You need a craft, or work in commerce, or be an employee to be able to sustain yourself. The land is not enough."

Suhaila got a high school degree from a coed school in their village, Kufur Tulth near Qalqilya. She had wanted to study English literature and *sharī'a* law, but her father could not pay for university. Therefore, she enrolled in a three-year midwifery diploma program at Ibn Sina College for Nursing because the fees were paid for by the Ministry of Health, pending work for the ministry for three years after graduation. Her parents sent her to midwifery school even though she would be on her own in another city: "They did not have much choice, nor did I really." She would have liked to get a BA in nursing/midwifery, but the Ministry of Health was only funding diplomas. Years later, she enrolled in a BA program while she was working and graduated in 2013.

She graduated with a diploma in midwifery in 1989. When she said so, I remarked, "Ok, so you were in Tulkarem schools when the First Intifada broke out?" "Yes," she replied, "we were in school. That was in '80 or '82.[10] I was in school. And the Second Intifada, I can't remember when that happened." I was baffled that she was mixing up the dates of the beginnings of both intifadas because these are such watershed dates in the contemporary history of Palestinians. Yet I said nothing, curious about what she would say next: "The intifada days are gone, now it is different. It is over. It has been decided and things have played themselves out (*inḥasmat*). There is something called intifada. This is history. A history that is gone." Here, Suhaila used a language that one commonly hears about the times of uprisings having passed. But I was still curious about her talking about the First Intifada being in 1980 or 1982.

She then shifted to talking about other watershed dates: "My mother used to tell me about the *hijra* of 1948 and 1960 the two Nakbas. How my grandmother was exiled, leaving my aunt, and then went back to get her." I interjected, quite confused: "You mean you were displaced?" She responded, "No, we are not refugees." Her family left their homes and went to their nearby land during the war, whether to flee or to protect their land, I did not know. Her grandmother, the story goes, left her aunt, who was an infant at home. Then she had to walk back through flying bullets to get her daughter and bring her to the fields where her family had camped out. Suhaila added, "They told me these stories, but we did not listen. My mom and dad lived during the Ottoman times. The Ottomans killed rebellious hearts. But I don't remember." I was confused by the jumbled narrative,

---

10. These were turbulent years in Palestine, with demonstrations against the turn of events in the war in Lebanon, against Menachem Begin's aggressive settlement policy, and against the deposing of pro-PLO mayors in most West Bank towns.

but she continued on, "People were scared and ran away. We always run away. We were scared. My father always said why did they leave their villages. But I say no one wants to witness crimes, killing, attacks on the honor of people, destruction of houses. One cannot witness this. A history of disasters. And now this is what is happening to Syrian people too. And to Iraqis." I stayed quiet for a while, and then she switched back to talking about the First Intifada in a realistic way, referring to dates, places, and precise anecdotes that refer to political events. She mentioned her age clearly and remembered a scene that many youngsters of the intifada would remember, demonstrations, stone throwing, and martyrs: "When the First Intifada started, I was twelve. My cousin and I were going to the baker to bake our bread. And the intifada had started. One young man was martyred that day. People were throwing stones and demonstrating; we were scared. And my cousin and I ran away. We ran away." Thus, the narrative had returned to the specificity typical of the oral history genre.

I was surprised by the breaks in the realism during the oral history recording. Why did she have trouble remembering when the First Intifada was and how old she was then? Why did she say "Ottomans killed rebellious hearts" in her discussion of her family's survival and escape tactics during the 1947–48 war? This sentence seems misplaced into the wrong story. It belongs to a type of storytelling practiced by an older generation, epic storytelling of heroes and adventures. At first, I thought I might ignore the few bits that did not fit with the overall realistic tone and voice in the oral history. But with time, I got used to realistic narratives switching to either confused speech, such as not remembering important dates, and poetic interjections, such as a sentence about the cruelty of the Ottomans. I came to think of this back and forth as characteristic of a transitional generation. The midwives were from poor rural or refugee families, often living in remote, marginalized villages or urban refugee camps. Many were between the ages of twenty-five and forty-five, and were the first literate generation and first to go to school in their families. As adults, the midwives worked in urban areas in centralized institutions such as hospitals and went back to their villages and camps on weekends. I see them as part of multiple communities and bridging several generations and social groups. They were fluent in both urbanized, professionalized ways of speaking, such as the oral history, and fluent in rural forms of storytelling, which peeked through during times of heightened emotion.

I started hearing in their speech the process described by Norbert Elias (1994) about manners and language changing over the course of generations, through what he called "the civilizing process." Schools, education, new forms of etiquette, and laws changed manners and language over centuries in Europe. Older forms of speech, popular language, and manners survived for a longer time among lower-class, rural, and marginalized communities. In the Levant, scholars have documented other forms of storytelling among an older, rural generation. Rosemary Sayigh (1998) observes that older women in refugee camps in Lebanon told stories (qiṣaṣ) that are fragmentary and particularistic. They are seldom framed in terms of a chronological narrative or a nationalist history; and because of this, are never considered history. Younger women, however, told sustained narratives about the self, structured by political events. I too observed that a younger generation of women told oral histories about the self. And paying close attention to the narratives showed breaks in the consistent narratives, such as "Ottomans killed rebellious hearts." Such sentences are fragments of older modes of storytelling, inserted into the realistic, recent oral history narrative.

The question then is why and when these sentences are inserted. And I suggest that such sentences appear in the oral history narrative at moments of recounting high emotion or stressful events. For Sohaila, it is after multiple shifts back and forth between confused story and realistic story around watershed political events, the intifada and the Nakba. At first, she forgot when the First Intifada was and how old she was. Then later, she remembered and told a realistic anecdote about it. She narrated a story about the Nakba and used an older terminology for that event, "exile," al-hijra. She was not alive during the Nakba and she is not from a refugee family. But she told a common story about the Nakba, about leaving a family member behind. At this point, she interjected a sentence about the Ottomans. Her narrative shows how sometimes, when life becomes messy, the narrative becomes messy.

After her shifts back and forth between different forms of speech, Suhaila returned to a narrative about being a working, struggling person, highlighting major chronological events. After receiving her diploma in midwifery, she had a contract with the Ministry of Health, to work for them for at least three years. She did so at the Jericho hospital, where she worked for four years. She would have liked to work near her village in Nablus, but the government did not agree because they needed staff in the Jericho hospital. After four years, she resigned and worked in the char-itable-nonprofit sector, first for three years at Red Crescent Hospital in Jerusalem, and then at Maqassed.

Suhaila emphasized how her experience in the workplace was part of a larger life history of struggle. "They treat you like you're a machine," she said, "They exploit you until the last drop of blood in your body. You work and work and work. You feel like it is all a struggle and it is taking a toll on your health." The closure has made her journey back and forth from her village to Jerusalem long and difficult. She struggles there as well. She suf-fers from not being near her parents, but there is no work near them. If she lived near her parents, she could have lunch with them and see her sisters. She would have more of a social life there than in Jerusalem, where it is very limited. Her anxiety is high because all she does is work and worry about her parents. She has few opportunities to socialize with her col-leagues because she works long days and is exhausted when she gets back to her dorm room at the end of the day. When I asked how she manages, she responded that she considers that she has spent her life struggling on her own. Then she corrected herself, "[My friends,] they are a beautiful thing in my life. They touched me. While I was studying, I would take my books to the labor room and my friends would cover for me so that I could study. I do not forget them. They are something beautiful in my life. They accompany me through life." But when she leaves one institution for the next, she leaves those friends behind. Thus, she feels like she has thin social support networks.

Her family has not always been supportive of her, although she sus-tains them financially. Part of her salary goes to her parents and buys necessary household items. She supports them more than her siblings do because she makes more money and because she does not have children. This is expected of her. Her married sisters have always lived on the edge financially, so she provides them small amounts of money on a regular basis. If someone in her family needs financial help, she steps in. For her brother to get married, she lent him ten thousand NIS. And now her father is in his seventies and continues to work at least two or three days a week in Israel. But still, it does not cover all the household needs. In any case, she says, "It is difficult not to give. You have to give. In the end you have to give." And giving is part of the inequalities in families. When her brother is in need, she gives to him. But if he were to see her in need one day, she doubts he would give to her: "If I grew old and then spent a few years in his house before I died, it should not be a problem. But there is no equal solidarity [takāful] in our families."

In her oral history, a strong sense of the independent, gendered individual emerged. Her family wanted her to marry, but she never did. One day her father told her that a man from her village had asked for her hand in marriage and that she should accept. But she refused because "he was not the right one for me." Her father got upset and demanded she stop working, and so she left Jericho hospital and returned to her village. She spent a week with her father at home until he calmed down and mended relationships with the family of the person who had asked for her hand in marriage. And after a week, he told her, "It seems you really don't want it, so go back to what you want to do." And she went back to her work in Jericho, proud of her independence.

Over the years, friends and family introduced her to many suitors, but she turned them all down:

> I consider that my naṣib [my chance or my share in life] has not arrived. To this day, I have not found the right person. And to this day, I say it clearly and openly, I am not willing to marry so that I can tell people I got married and console society . . . If I die unmarried, it is ok. At least I would not have made a mistake and married someone who is not appropriate for me. For society, you have to have a family, a husband. So that you don't remain alone, they tell you. Your mom and dad are going to die, they tell you. But I'm not willing to get married in order to not

be lonely. I have friends for that. My faith in god has increased, and I believe in *naṣib*. If there is *naṣib*, god will bring it to us. My friends, it is different. They are important because I can't live alone.

She continues, "They tell you that you should marry for financial independence, but it is not men or children who give women financial independence . . . A man does not empower a woman, finances do. It is after I had worked for years and suffered from work and seen the gains that I realized how important work was to independence." Thus, like in Tahrir's oral history, a strong sense of the gendered, independent self emerges where work and financial independence are more highly valued than the gendered expectations of society.

The last time I saw her, she was still working at the Jerusalem hospital and returned to her village every three weeks. She wondered whether she could do a master's degree in midwifery. With an MA, she would be paid more and could possibly combine teaching with practice. She had bought land in her village and was planning to build a house. She was proud of her property. She was the only woman in her family who owned land on her own, she told me.

In this chapter, I narrated the oral histories of Tahrir and Suhaila, which I recorded in their dorm rooms. Each has a unique life history, and while they share a profession and work, their backgrounds and trajectories are different. The narratives are characteristic of the oral history genre. The narrative arc, plot, and tone are typical of oral histories of their generations and social context. They underlined their everyday struggles with the closure, exploitative work, and strained family relations, as well as the places, dates, and political events that structured their oral history. However, ethnographic attention reveals moments of disjunction in their narratives. For Tahrir, the ruptures in her narrative indexed the high emotionality and struggle she experienced while being separated from her children. I never understood how many years they were removed from her or how she managed to bring them back. For Suhaila, who was from a more rural and underserved community, the disjunctive stories I heard were mixtures of multiple genres of speech, the chronologically ordered oral history narrative and the lyrical genre of stories spoken by an older rural generation. Over the course of my fieldwork, I came to identify oral histories as rich sources of data not only because of their consistency and flow, but because the disruptions in the narratives reflect fissures and social change.

3

A History of Oral History

Palestinian oral history is a decentralized and well-circulated medium, unlike most post-colonial oral history projects generated by a state. In this chapter, I reread published Palestinian oral history collections and observe the changes in the genre over the years, especially as they pertain to the subjects of oral history. In the 1970s, 1980s, and 1990s, the literature focused on rebellions, peasants, refugees, and destroyed villages. More recently, oral history has come to focus on the politically active, gendered, and working person as subject. Most importantly, in the oral history genre, a strong sense of the individual voice and its history emerges.

Because of oral history's wide circulation, coupled with its political salience, young, working women carved a niche for themselves and used the genre to talk about the kinds of challenges and political and social work they were doing. In my fieldwork, midwives used the oral history format to talk about their struggles and lives. As seen in the previous chapter, the oral histories presented a strong sense of the gendered self, with a common narrative arc and plot. Yet brothers and husbands did not offer to give oral histories. On the contrary, they made short remarks about being fed up with everything. They did not feel that oral history was an effective mode for presenting themselves.

In the midwives' oral histories, women from a poor background with an education and a low-paid job have strong individual voices, presenting themselves as somewhat independent of male kin, and years later indicating that they are upwardly mobile. Indeed, in longitudinal work, midwives with whom I had conducted oral history interviews years earlier used the phrase "we were steadfast" (ṣamadna) to describe their state of being over the years and to explain how they were doing better socially, economically, and psychologically than they had been. As they carved a niche for themselves in the genre of oral history and as they displayed their upward mobility to me and to people around them, midwives, teachers, and other low-paid women workers contributed to the shaping of a desirable type of classed femininity in an increasingly precarious political and economic context.

Spreading Oral History

Oral history is a prominent and visible narrative form in Palestine; it is used by scholars and laypeople for various types of projects and audiences (scholarly, educational, archival, legal, familial, heritage, artistic). Contemporary scholars of the Israel-Palestine war frame the history as either ethnic cleansing or settler colonialism. The first positions the war in the history of ethnic cleansing and displacement, making connections to the Shoah (the Hebrew word, meaning "catastrophe," is used among historians to refer to the Holocaust), the Armenian genocide, and ethnic cleansing in Bosnia-Herzegovina (Allen 2013; Slyomovics 1998; Davis 2011). In Susan Slyomovics's work on memory and a Palestinian village in Israel, her genealogy of the "memorial book" documenting the destroyed village begins with Armenians who fled their villages between 1917 and 1924. It continues through the experience of Eastern European Jews who survived the Holocaust and fled their countries between 1939 and 1945, then through the experience of Palestinians who fled their villages between 1948 and 1950. Finally, it investigates the experience of Bosnians who fled between 1990 and 1992. Slyomovics shows how these forms of documentation, and this kind of memory work, is common to post-ethnic cleansing contexts.

The second framing, now common in contemporary scholarship, is that of settler colonialism. Julie Peteet's ethnography of space and mobility in Palestine frames the story of the war as a Zionist project that dispossesses the indigenous population, isolates villages, towns, and cities, and immobilizes them in enclaves (Peteet 2017, 3). This framing tells the story of Palestine as one of displacement, akin to the Indigenous populations in the United States, Canada, and Australia, for example. However, when Palestinian oral history emerged in the early 1970s, the Palestine

Liberation Organization (PLO) and political culture, in general, thought of its struggle more like the anti-colonial struggles of the Algerian Front de Libération Nationale, the Libyan resistance movement to Italian colonization, the South Vietnamese National Liberation Front, and liberation struggles in Portuguese Africa than to the experience of Indigenous populations in the Americas or Australia. In fact, PLO officials rejected the comparisons made by scholars and students in Palestine with the Native American experience because they wanted to make connections with colonized peoples who have strong national liberation movements. The PLO thought of the war as a colonial one and their struggle as an anti-colonial and national movement. This was reinforced by key cadres of the PLO, forming political and economic relationships with Ben Bella and Algerian leaders at independence in 1962, and later with Libya (a relationship that dwindled and then came to a halt in 1977), as well as legendary leaders of the Cuban liberation struggle, such as Che Guevara (Sayigh 1997, 102).

The diplomatic relationships were reinforced by Libyan and Algerian financial aid to the PLO. After 1977, this aid extended to some leftist parties, such as the Democratic Front for the Liberation of Palestine.[1] It also included training militias and, importantly, hiring thousands of Palestinians, especially as school teachers, health system workers, and staff in political and cultural organizations (Sayigh 1997, 102). Such political alliances and work opportunities during this time coincided with the emergence of oral history projects for many newly independent post-colonial nations. The Jihad Center for Libyan Studies (founded in 1977) had a Jihad Oral History Center. Its mission was to record and transcribe the history

1. The PLO, following the model of nearly all anti-colonial liberation struggles, was subject to repeated factional divisions and subdivisions, based always on a combination of ideological and personal considerations. The Democratic Front for the Liberation of Palestine (DFLP, originally DPFLP), led by Nayef Hawatmeh, split off from George Habash's Popular Front for the Liberation of Palestine in 1968, ostensibly based on a Marxist critique of the dominant line (itself proclaiming a Marxist-Leninist, pan-Arab rejection of Arafat's rather nonideological and purely Palestinian nationalism). In the longer term, the DFLP also experienced an internal split, a sizeable portion of its cadres supporting Arafat and the Oslo Accord of 1993.

of surviving Libyans who resisted Italian occupation between 1911 and 1943. Soon thereafter, Algeria, Tunisia, and Morocco also created oral history centers (Ahmida 1994). There was an imperative on the part of the new nation-state to record the oral histories of political resistance from peasants and working-class people, as a counterpoint to colonial archives that recorded the lives of elites and notables. Palestinian oral history efforts emerged at the same time as these other state projects, and it is this anti-colonial frame that influenced its beginnings.

However, unlike these national contexts, oral history in Palestine was not produced or collected by a state institution or a political party. And maybe because it was not a statist project, it left room for people to appropriate it. The medium spread quickly. From amongst these many Arab post-colonial experiences, the Palestinian oral history effort remains a major body of literature in the field. This is, in part, because Palestinian oral history was a local, decentralized, grassroots endeavor led by scholars, community activists, village councils, charities, and non-governmental organizations. Rosemary Sayigh (2002) explains the emergence of oral history inside Israel and the Occupied Territories, and then in the diaspora, as encompassing the different political cultures in which Palestinians lived:

> For that generation [adults in 1967] in the Arab diaspora, at a time of mounting Arab nationalism, there did not appear an immediate danger of losing Palestinian history. When later, and with great difficulty, NCIs [national cultural institutions] were formed by Palestinian communities in Israel–Yafa, al-Taybeh-Nazareth, Shafa Amr, and Rohat, a different political and cultural context produced different aims. Living under a dominant system that was more alien and hostile than the Arab host regimes, NCIs and individual intellectuals in Israel have been more "conservationist" in their work, for example in the "reconstruction" of the destroyed villages, for which they have utilized oral testimonies and topography. (Sayigh 2002, 3)

In the beginning, individual researchers in Israel, unsupported by institutions, started recording oral histories of villages. Then, group-recording projects were put together and community-based organizations started recording oral histories. Sometimes, village councils commissioned and funded village studies based on oral histories (Slyomovics 1998, 223). The first such institutional project was the work of a nongovernmental organization called In'āsh Al-'Usra. It started a project of recording rural traditions after the occupation of the West Bank in 1967, producing the first of the village studies on Termosa'iyya (In'āsh Al-'Usra 1973). Thereafter, Birzeit University's Arab Documentation and Research Center started an oral history project led by Sharif Kanaana and Bassam Kaabi and began publishing the *Destroyed Palestinian Villages* series. Indeed, many of the early oral histories were about the destroyed villages and the experience of displacement.

In the meantime, Nafez Nazzal and Rosemary Sayigh published two influential books. Nafez Nazzal's pathbreaking book, *The Palestinian Exodus from Galilee: 1948* (1978), analyzes oral history interviews with Palestinian refugees in Beirut and their narratives of expulsion and the period of departure from their villages in the Galilee. At the same time, Rosemary Sayigh published her landmark book, *From Peasants to Revolutionaries* (1979), which analyzes oral histories of refugees in Lebanon and traces their exodus and grouping into refugee camps. These works foregrounded later works that focused on how the refugee camp gradually became the symbol of expulsion and the site for the forging of new identities (Sayigh 1994; Peteet 1991; Allan 2013). Then, during the First Intifada (1987–91), Adel Yahya, influenced by Sayigh's book and the teaching of Tom Ricks at Birzeit University (Heacock 2018), started training students and community activists in oral history methods. As part of this process, starting in 1990 he published the first of a series of oral history methods books, mainly in Arabic (Yahya 1990a, 1990b, 1999a, 1999b, 2002, 2006; Yahya, Mahmud, and Ricks 1994). These books were widely circulated as pamphlets in schools, universities, and among politically active young people.

Some of the oral history projects during that period were conducted as PhD or MA theses and were the work of individual students. Nafez Nazzal (1974) and Sonia Nimr (1990) were some of the earliest PhD theses using oral history to document Palestinian history. Less well-known theses were produced in the History Department at Gaza Islamic University. And some of the oral history projects from the 1980s were large, group projects involving many interviewers. These included In'ash al-Usra, Birzeit University Documentation Center; Sahera Dirbas in the Galilee; and Adel Yahya in the West Bank. Each of these large oral history projects involved a lead researcher and many fieldworkers. The fieldworkers were often students or employees of organizations who received training in oral history methods and conducted trial interviews with people in their vicinity, like shopkeepers or public figures, before being sent to other field sites to conduct interviews.

During the 1990s, many oral history projects continued to emerge. The Gaza Community Mental Health Project, led by Iyyad Al-sarraj, had a Nakba recording project. In the Palestinian diaspora in Syria, where there were few NGOs, a publishing house in Al-Yarmuk camp, Dar al-Shajara, started publishing written oral histories (Bash 1998; Al-Hardan 2016). Al-Jana (ARCPA) in Lebanon published several oral histories, especially focused on youth education; the *Journal of Palestine Studies* had an oral history issue; and the Welfare Association began a Memory Museum. Since 2000, Diana Allan and Mahmoud Zeidan co-founded the "Nakba Archive," an audio and video recording repository of experiences of 1948. In 2003 Ted Swedenburg published a book based on earlier oral history work about the great Arab revolt, which had been of central interest to researchers in the late 1980s as they recorded elderly survivors' oral histories before they died (Heacock 2018; Nimr 1990). And since 2006, the American University of Beirut launched the Palestinian Oral History Project.

If oral history was not produced by the state or an institution as is usually the case, then who are the oral historians of Palestine? The oral historians are heterogeneous in their training and work. Most are Palestinian. A few are American or European researchers who are in solidarity with the Palestinian cause. Many are scholars: Rosemary Sayigh, Sharif Kanaana, Randa Farah, Sonia Nimr, Thomas Ricks, May Saikaly, the late Adel Yahya, Susan Slyomovics, Saleh Abdel-Jawad, and Ted Swedenburg. A number had a connection to Birzeit University at different points in their lives. Others were independent scholars. And yet others work in NGOs. Another group of oral historians are not academics. Sahera Dirbas is a writer and filmmaker. Jamil Arafat is a retired school director. They are in various occupations and much of their work in oral history grew out of personal experience, growing up in a dispossessed community in 1948 or with refugee status in the diaspora. Their observations of collective loss generated the curiosity and mission to recover the unwritten past (Sayigh 2002, 66). In addition to being part of a dispossessed community and having refugee status, another impetus for oral history was the feeling that history was being written by elites and that the poor (refugee and peasant) were excluded from such histories (Sayigh 1979, 2002).

The oral history projects sought to preserve elements of rural life thought to be disappearing. Oral historians were part of a wider interest in rural ways of life or folklore, among poets, musicians, artists, and heritage organizations during the 1970s and 1980s. In response to the occupation of the West Bank and Gaza of 1967, In'āsh Al-'Usra founded the Research Committee for Social and Palestinian Popular Heritage (later renamed Center for Palestinian Popular Heritage). Since then, the center has been publishing research about proverbs, stories, songs, and oral traditions in a specialized magazine, *Al-Turāth wa-l Mujtama'* (Heritage and Society). The Popular Arts' Center (*Markiz al-Funūn al-Sha'bīyya*) recorded hundreds of hours of traditional songs and produced two CDs based on this work.[2]

Indeed, Palestinian national discourse glorified peasant life and living closely attached to the land.[3] Ted Swedenburg (1990) has discussed the Palestinian peasant as a national signifier. The themes of refugees and peasants are connected in the popular history of Palestine because colonization,

---

2. The first CD was titled *Zaghareed: A Palestinian Wedding* and appeared in 1990.

3. Rosemary Sayigh (2015) and Laleh Khalili (2004) noted that the PLO in the 1960s and 1970s showed interest in the peasantry because they held the Vietnamese and Algerian anti-colonial struggles as models, but were not genuinely interested in knowing about peasant experiences and lives. This is an important observation, especially in paying attention to the fraught relationship between the PLO and refugees in the diaspora, many of whom are of peasant background. However, in the case of oral historians and other researchers, filmmakers, and artists, especially in Israel and the Occupied Territories, they studied some aspects of rural ways of life seriously, as illustrated by the films, music, folklore collections, and published oral histories of the time.

displacement, and occupation were central to the shift from agricultural economies to wage labor. Thus, oral history has been, in large part, a concerted effort to preserve rural and refugee culture. Palestinian oral history has focused on peasant and refugee narratives and the medium both reflects and constructs particular types of subjects that remember, value, and think of themselves through those kinds of experiences, thereby erasing or downplaying other kinds of histories and experiences.

Scholars such as Adel Yahya were important in spreading oral history as a genre of speech and writing. Yahya not only produced an oral history archive and a written oral history on refugees but also produced a manual for the oral historian in Arabic, accessible to a literate public (Yahya 1990, 2002). In the manual, he sees oral history work as a communal project that involves a group of people, lead researchers, fieldworkers, transcribers, editors, and people with knowledge about a historical period or problem. He saw the projects as a way to "preserve the heritage of the Palestinian people," which was the title of one of the projects he led. He traveled in the Arab world to lecture and conduct workshops about the uses of oral history in refugee communities and in postwar environments, such as in Iraq after the Gulf War, and he was surprised to discover that countries such as Egypt, Iraq, and Gulf countries, with important universities, did not have oral history archives or projects in place (Yahya 2002, 32).

For him, oral history was a means for political survival. He thought of it as a way to preserve culture from being erased and to resist efforts to Judaize and de-Arabize places and practices in the Occupied Territories. During this time, narrating oral history and other forms of witnessing became an urgent national Palestinian imperative, widely considered a political survival mechanism. But Yahya also saw it as necessary in a national context, in order to bring out local histories and make stories in the press and scholarship more complex through the narratives of disadvantaged communities. He promoted the method as useful for Arab countries to preserve heritage and the memory of political upheavals and to give voice to diverse and unequal communities. Yahya continuously presented his team's work in camps and villages in the central West Bank, where he lived, practiced, and contributed to its spread.

Furthermore, because oral history targeted a diverse audience, not only scholars in a specialized field but a wider lay public, oral history facilitated a political role for scholarly writing. Oral history was a type of writing that could be used to contribute to the discipline and profession of history, anthropology, or folklore. It could also be used in consciousness-raising pamphlets to educate people about village details that existed, why and how people fled, and local/rural traditions. This position between scholarly writing and the political pamphlet, both well-developed and circulated genres in Palestine, gave oral historians a role as engaged intellectuals. The interlocutors in the oral histories usually spoke about being refugees and peasants. The form was located between a pamphlet and an academic book. Both the subjects of the study and the form connected closely to the political movements of the time. And because Palestinian oral history was not part of a state project, people appropriated and used the medium in different ways from the 1970s through the 2000s.

Shifts in the Subjects of Oral History: From Refugee and Peasant to the Urban, Struggling, Gendered Person

Since the second intifada in 2000, there has been a shift in the focus of oral histories and ethnographies. Gendered and urban experiences, as well as the experiences of a younger generation, take center stage (for example, see Collins 2004; Allen 2006; Allan 2013). The younger generation was not alive during the Nakba and often lives or works in urban environments with an omnipresent national movement. There seems to be a shift in focus from displaced, rural peasant to urban, marginalized, struggling, and working person. The shift has been observed by oral historians and anthropologists in different ways. Rosemary Sayigh notes a difference in narrative genres between elderly and younger women: elderly, unschooled women told stories (*qiṣaṣ*) with particular aesthetics and narratives, characterized by "hesitancy/plural subject/discontinuity pattern," whereas the pattern of younger women's narrations was "readiness to speak, the singular subject, and autonomous narratives referenced to nationalist history" (Sayigh 2007, 149). Diana Allan (2007) has discussed the politics of Nakba commemoration in Shatila refugee camp and traces how the camp youth negotiate public remembrance and push her to focus on recent images of rebellion rather than those of the Nakba. Lori Allen (2013) has noted the way her informants discussed the emotion of *zahaq*, being "fed up" by the continuing violence and lack of end to the conflict. Ruba Salih (2018) noticed a generational shift from telling the history of the village of origin to telling the history of the camp amongst Palestinian refugees in the Occupied Territories.

In my reading of Adel Yahya's published collections of oral histories, elderly men tell the history of villages, camps, tribes, and states with a mixture of journalistic language and language from epic poetry. On the other hand, younger women tell a sustained narrative about the self with references to dates, massacres, political events, and precise places, with a particular emotional tone and force, grieving over the loss of a child, for example, but also pushing the younger generation to political commitment. Rural and urban women, inhabitants of cities and younger working people carve a niche for themselves in oral history. Indeed, in my own fieldwork starting in 2002, young, refugee, and rural working-class women told oral histories. Doctors and upper-class men and women, on the other hand, usually produced other genres of witnessing. Some produced memoirs, either in text or in film (Barghouthi 2005).[4] Others narrated the oral history of an institution or political movement, but not a life history. Some of these institutional oral histories appear in chapter 4.

As narrated in the stories of Tahrir, Suhaila, and others, the nurses and midwives were excellent users of the oral history genre. They told sustained narratives of the self. The emplotment of their lives was romantic (White 1973). They began with stories about life in poverty and struggling alongside their parents and older siblings; the stories continued with continuously working and struggling at work and at home; and they ended with an unfinished story about exhaustion and the need to continue. One way the speakers presented themselves as having a strong gendered

---

4. The literature on Palestinian memoirs from different periods and locations is rich and diverse. See, for example, Jabra (1995); Tamari (2003); Salam-Khalidi (1978); Tuqan (1990); Sakakini (2003); Amiry (2004); and Darwish (2013).

sense of self was by talking about deploying a constant low-level energy to struggle, which they sometimes called *sumud* (steadfastness), or they used other words from the lexicon of struggle. Suhaila, who was not politically active, talked about her life and work as a long struggle: "You feel like it is all a struggle [*kifāḥ bi kifāḥ ou niḍāl fi niḍāl*] and it takes a toll on your health." The midwives talked about everyday struggles against occupation, in their workplace, and in their families.

Ghassan Hage, in his observations of Palestine, described practices he saw as part of the category of "resilience," which he distinguished from "resistance." Resistance has a tragic dimension that damages the political and social fabric of society, and it is exhausting because of the repression, surveillance, and form of politics it entails (Hage 2013). Resilience, on the other hand, involves endurance not deformed by occupation as a specific Palestinian mode of existence.[5] In the oral histories of the midwives, they repeatedly referenced the endurance that their lives required of them.

In addition to presenting their lives as stories of constant struggle against occupation, exploitation from their jobs, and mistreatment in their families and marriages, the midwives explicitly talked about themselves as being a new generation of women. They were educated and worked on the market; some did not marry, and others divorced. Furthermore, they talked of a change in the way women thought of themselves. In Tahrir's

---

5. Recent literature on sumud has broken some of the romantic associations of the word. Moghnieh 2021 discusses its connections to psychological notions of trauma and its embeddedness in the cultural semantics of psychological experiences in Lebanon. Segal 2016 explores the boundaries between endurance and exhaustion in Palestine and the ways in which exhaustion manifests itself in families. In a different kind of media, a video produced on the anniversary of the Beirut Port explosion of August 4, 2020, by the alternative media organization *Megaphone*, the video talked about *la'nat assumūd*, "the curse of sumud," in Lebanon. This phrase enabled discussion of the ways in which people slowly reconstructed their lives and adapted to the post-explosion society, unable to change the political leadership. In the video footage of *habbat al-Quds*, the Jerusalem uprising of 2021, demonstrators and singers used the terms "revolution" (*thawra*) and "freedom" (*hurrīyya*), thus connecting themselves to the Arab Spring. Among the books published by the Institute for Palestine Studies, I noticed many recent authors were using *albaqā'*, "remaining," or "survival," in their works. See, for example, Mannaa (2016); Malki (2018); and Jo'beh (2021).

oral history interview, for example, she stresses how important financial independence is to her life story:

> You know there is something about Arab women. They used to give to their children and husbands and be satisfied. It is not like today. A long time ago, they used to abuse themselves because they gave so much. . . . Today, it is not the same thing. Our generation today, like me for example: my relationship with my husband. If he is abusive and I can separate from him, I can do it and I will do it. Women think differently now. It is no longer that I give and I give and we remain master and slave. I am not willing to work inside and outside and then listen to "go to your father's house" or endure him hitting me. . . . Women used to be much more patient [taṣbur]. Maybe because they would be scared for the children . . . where would they go? Even if she took her children, where would she bring them up?

Thus, Tahrir saw her generation as different from her mother's because many women of her generation work and have an income. In addition, she and other midwives talked about their mothers' generation as being more "patient," which is not surprising, as ṣabr, or "patience is a virtue" is often attributed to women and the elderly. Tahrir sees a fundamental change in the character of women of her generation. Suhaila, likewise, pointed to similar changes, worded a bit differently. She talked about herself and other young women as more assabiyya (short-tempered) than older women.

Younger women narrated their own lives as individual, struggling persons distinct from their foremothers, who did not have an official, full-time, and respected wage work. They also portrayed themselves as distinct from the men of their generations in their families, who were often less educated and either underemployed or unemployed. The midwives described themselves as independent, financially and psychologically. Together, their narratives characterize their uniquely modern existence as women and main breadwinners of families.

While the nurses and midwives told detailed narratives about the self, their brothers and husbands rarely did so. The brothers and husbands often told stories or made short remarks about being fed up. Many men were unemployed or had occasional temporary work and most had to live in the circumscribed spaces of their villages or camps. Indeed, the severe closure since the beginning of the Second Intifada in 2000 had gendered effects on the wage labor market. Historically, the 1967 occupation of the West Bank and Gaza simultaneously undermined the Palestinian economy (agricultural and small manufacturing) and allowed Palestinians, mainly male day workers, access to the labor market inside Israel. During the 1990s, the number of Palestinian workers in Israel was reduced (Farsakh 2005) and, since 2000, it has been greatly reduced. Furthermore, labor migration opportunities in the Gulf States have gradually receded. Thus, the economy has become more reliant on foreign aid and more precarious, exhibiting high rates of unemployment (Mitchell 2010). Consequently, more women have been seeking wage labor, especially in the fields of teaching, nursing, and government jobs.

Telling a story with a narrative arc similar to the histories of gender during the world wars and during the Algerian War of Independence, a report issued in 2010 by FAFO (a Norwegian research foundation) writes of "women's advance and men's retreat in the labor force" (Mitchell 2010, 27). Indeed, the author of the report sees women seeking wage labor as a coping strategy, trying to augment household income amid economic crisis (see also Al-Botmeh and Sotnik [2007] for another account). Additionally, she notes the despair experienced by male interviewees and practices that rendered them "invisible" to their own communities, making it difficult for them to handle their unemployment and dependency on their family members for various forms of income generation (Mitchell 2010). I suggest that the nurses and midwives insisted that I record their oral history because they worked, struggled, and felt productive. One interpretation is that young men may have been uninterested in my research on birth and medicine. But I think that more likely they did not feel that they had an oral history that was worthwhile to tell.

The young men's distaste for oral history was particularly visible during lunch at a visit to a midwife's home in a remote and underserved village in the Ramallah area. The midwife's father, who was the village sheikh, started criticizing his son for wanting to remarry. The son interjected that he was sick and tired of life in his village. He was unemployed, his father explained in front of him. He had worked in the Gulf for a few years but then fell out of work and returned to his village to find the closure at its height. He could neither find work nor leave his village. He lived with his wife, who was from his village, and they had three children. He was so bored and sick and tired of his life and wanted to find a way out, but was always confronted by a brick wall because of the lack of employment and the strict closure. He thought he could marry again (taking a second wife), but felt he needed to get out of his community and village for such a step to be interesting. So he had to just keep on doing what he was doing. During this conversation, the son was mainly quiet, listening. His father and sister were vocally critical of him.

His sister, who had just gotten married and was pregnant, was an experienced midwife working in a Ramallah hospital where she was likewise critical of the classist discourse of doctors and city people. She said that she married someone uneducated, but that they had an understanding of what they wanted from each other. It was a marriage brokered by their families. They had gotten to know each other and loved each other and had agreed on each spouse's duties, responsibilities, and rights. She said that work in the market was a central responsibility of hers and that her marriage was smooth because he was from her village, and they had agreed on these issues beforehand.

Her father ended the discussion by saying, "You see, best is to marry from your own community." I tried a number of times afterwards to chat with Rabi', but he was not interested. And finally, once, he said, "You know for your research, you should focus on my sister." The brothers and husbands of midwives were often uninterested and sometimes actively indifferent to my research.[6] Women, on the other hand, were often eager to give oral history interviews because the medium highlighted them as valuable persons who work, struggle, and manage things well.

Discussions about marriage were moments when midwives declared the importance of their independence clearly. As seen in chapter 3, Suhaila,

---

6. This was not the case for all men. Some took interest in my research, helped me get access to hospitals, and provided me with oral history narratives. These were mainly doctors or nurses. Often, the male nurses had wives who worked as nurses too.

who was unmarried, discussed marriage for a long time in her oral history and made it clear that her independence, financial and otherwise, was essential to who she was:

> A long time ago, I did not know how important financial issues were to women's power. A man does not empower a woman, finances do. It is after I had worked for a number of years and suffered from work and seen the gains that I realized how important finances are to independence.
>
> And actually for that [support], marriage is not a guarantee. Many married women have husbands who marry a second wife or leave them and stop asking about them. If a wife gets terminally ill, most probably she will go back to her parents. There are many instances where a husband is not a good guarantee.
>
> I wish I had a master's degree. But my conditions of life make it hard for me right now. I am tired. I used to take shifts one after the other in order to go to college. I would go to my parents only once every five months so that I can study. I was so pressured. My plan for when I can, is to get an MA degree. Then maybe I can teach at a university, less tiring job. A husband is not everything. I don't like women who think that the husband is everything. Who think that if you don't have a husband you are nothing.

In these quotes, Suhaila speaks about why she thinks marriage is not essential and can be detrimental to women's lives. She thinks of financial independence as more important than marriage. In thinking about her future, marriage is not part of her scheme. She plans to further her education and find a less tiring job. She articulates a strong sense of self and of why independence is essential to a decent life.

Femininity Somewhat Disengaged from Male Kin

In the oral histories, a unique individual emerges with distinctive moral and mental characteristics not simply indicative of their national belonging or class, but rather of their own personal subjectivity. Oral history encourages interviewees to tell a sustained narrative about the self and to understand their own stories through the lens of the individual, assimilating their own histories into the present circumstances and integrating their present circumstances into their pasts. This process is instrumental in the formation and spread of oral history as a genre and in its distinction from history, which tells the stories of nations and leaders, and storytelling, which narrates fictional and fabulous events. Furthermore, oral histories of younger women, such as those I examine here, contribute to a new kind of gendered life trajectory where the interlocutor from a poor background gets an education, and then works and struggles over time to become upwardly mobile and economically independent.

I observed the upward mobility of many nurses and midwives in my longitudinal work. After my extended fieldwork in 2002, 2003, and 2004, I visited them every other year until 2018. Over the course of the years, I observed changes in their living arrangements and belongings. In January 2008, four years after the initial oral history interview, I met with Tahrir in a hospital lobby. She was still working and managing her relationship with her ex-husband, with whom the children lived and saw her on weekends. She told me that she had just seen her children and that her daughter had marks on her head from her father's beating. Calling the domestic violence help line was ridiculous because they did not have the executive power needed to enforce protection. But she still hoped that she could give her daughter strength whenever she saw her.

On another return visit in 2014, Tahrir insisted I visit her in her home this time. Her living arrangements had changed again. She had moved out of her parents' home, a ground-floor cement structure with a living room, kitchenette, and two adjacent bedrooms, and rented an apartment outside the camp, a move signifying upward mobility. Her second-floor apartment was cozy, with tile flooring covered with carpets and light coming through the windows. Her children now lived with her. Two were in university and one was in secondary school. Her husband had a new family, worked as a taxi driver when he had work, and no longer tormented them, although she said he remained important for legal decisions such as their children's marriages. She provided everything for her children. When I arrived, she had just gone to the neighboring hills to pick *za'tar* (thyme): "You see," she told me, as I walked in the house, "*ṣamaḍna*, we persevered." Her living conditions and her children being in college and no longer living with their father indicated that she was now more financially comfortable than she had been the last time I visited her.

While midwives were overworked, and compared to doctors underpaid, there was always demand for their labor. During my fieldwork, hospital administrators would entice midwives to leave their work at one hospital and come work at another hospital for better pay or more benefits. Whenever one of the midwives resigned, I would find her a few days later working at another hospital. Demand for midwifery care meant they were steadily employed and receiving salaries over decades, which improved their living conditions. For example, when I visited Suhaila in 2013, she told me she had saved enough money over her years of hard work at the hospital to buy land in her village. Her family was harvesting part of that land, and on another part, she was hoping to build a small house. She said she was the first woman in her village to own land on her own.

What is also important in the midwives' upward mobility is how it is visible to me and to people around them. Tahrir and others posted pictures of their children at college on their Facebook accounts and on the public social media account of their camp or village. Villagers who came to the hospital as patients spoke about the land Suhaila had bought and the house she was going to build. The visibility of their upward mobility contributes to the construction and appeal of this new kind of femininity that is financially and psychologically independent.

The assertion of individual female subjectivity in this context indicates the psychological development of gendered, modern subjectivities (Katz 1990; Massad 2007) of an independent and autonomous female that can exist somewhat disengaged from kin relations with men. Tahrir, for example, mentions that her husband is no longer present in her life, nor in the lives of her children, although she notes that they will need him for legal transactions. Suhaila is imagining a future unmarried, building a house on her land in her village where she will live when she retires. Through oral histories, these women rewrite domestic practices and present a femininity that is desirable and realistic for lower-middle-class, educated women.

The nineteenth-century British novel presented fictional characters as unique individuals with distinctive moral and mental characteristics not indicative of their class or status, but rather of their own personal subjectivity. Nancy Armstrong (1987) examines the way the texts instruct the reader to read about proper emotional reactions, domestic behavior, and sexual practices. She argues that modern culture depends on a form of power that works through language and, in particular, the printed word, to constitute subjectivity. As a result, the novel provided the impetus for the rise of the middle class. I argue here that oral histories, in ways similar to the novel in nineteenth-century Britain, have contributed to shaping a desirable and worthy form of femininity that is somewhat independent from male kin.

Historians of gender and sexuality have been attentive to how moments of crisis and war change the workforce, opening up spaces for women to take on new economic, social, and political roles. Allan Berube (1983), for example, documents the mass movement of women from small towns in the United States to cities during World War II to fill manufacturing positions, giving them opportunities unforeseen by the system to break out from domesticated roles of daughters, wives, and mothers, getting to know themselves and other women on different terms, transforming norms of gender and sexuality.

Economic processes such as the shift to wage labor and the rise of the middle class are also often credited with transformations in family structures (Collier 1986). To this end, it is important also to explore the media that accompany such economic changes and the influence they have on concepts of self and family. Scholars have written about the powerful discursive forces of human rights (Allen 2013) and trauma (Fassin 2008) on Palestinian political subjectivity. Yet the force of oral history on local audiences, and for constructing strong, individual, and gendered subjects has been underestimated. This may be because it is considered an academic (sub)field with a Western audience. Far from being removed from historical and political events, I argue that the spread of the oral historical form in Palestine not only constitutes subjectivities, but also reflects the rise of an educated working class in which women, often employed as teachers and nurses, are the family breadwinners.

In the first chapter, I talked about birth as a moment of loss for young women who had moved to their husbands' villages and were not able to visit their parents or families of origin as they cared for their newborns. I used Suad Joseph's insight about "connective selves," where subjectivity is enmeshed and connected to male kin and patriarchy, to explain the disarray they felt when they had to rearrange connective relationships. Suad Joseph positions families as "one of the most powerful social structures throughout the Arab world" (Joseph 2018, 1), around which the social, political, economic, and religious pivot. Still, Joseph discourages an essentialized understanding of the term, as families are constantly "invented and reinvented" (Joseph 2010, 47).[7] This encourages me to think of the emergent families the midwives present in their narratives with women as main breadwinners. In this chapter, I argue that the midwives present a narrative in the oral histories of a gendered person with a strong sense of self, who is largely disengaged from male kin.

Joseph proposes the term "patriarchal connectivity" to describe the interplay of gender, selves, and identity in her understanding of family in the Arab World. Patriarchal connectivity is a system that produces selves with "fluid boundaries organized for gendered and aged domination in a culture that valorizes kin structures, morality, and idioms" (Joseph 1999, 12). Joseph thus sees persons as entrenched in relational networks that shape their deepest sense of self. However, she simultaneously alerts us to the fact that these selves are distinctive, with each having its own initiative and agency whose autonomy is, nonetheless, constrained by the confluence of patriarchy and connectivity. Here Joseph understands patriarchy as a set of cultural constructs and structural relations that place men and elders in a position to direct the lives of others. Furthermore, connectivity is understood as a set of cultural constructs and structural relations where individuals invite and require an involvement with others to shape the self (Joseph 1999). Thus, the familial self is a non-essentialized active agent, always in flux and distinct from the "western homogenized individual-bounded, self-contained, and autonomous [self]" (Joseph 1999, 15). Here, I suggest that midwives fit Joseph's articulation of connective selves, but

---

7. See also Doumani (2003) for an analysis of the diversity of family forms and practices, as well as the very meaning of the term.

throughout their lives and often after decades of working, they depart from it and narrate themselves as having a subjectivity largely disengaged from male kin.

The midwives used romance in their oral histories to talk about their lives of constant struggle and the construction of independent lives. They used the concept of sumud and it worked to describe their lives because it does not have the tragic trajectory of resistance (Hage 2013). In her famous article, Lila Abu-Lughod (1990) cautioned scholars not to let themselves be absorbed by "the romance of resistance." But what does one do when the interlocutors themselves use romance to understand their stories?

Conclusion

In this chapter, I explored the history of Palestinian oral history. When the genre emerged, the Palestinian national movement thought of the war as a colonial war and their struggle as anti-colonial, with a strong movement similar to independence movements in Asia and Africa, many of which had instituted large state-run oral history projects. However, unlike the oral history projects of newly independent postcolonial countries, Palestinian oral history was not a state project. It was a decentralized effort. Starting in the 1970s, independent intellectuals, village councils, teachers, and their students practiced oral history. The medium spread quickly. Oral history was distributed as pamphlets in schools and workshops.

The oral historians were conservationists and wanted to preserve local traditions and experiences. They thought of traditional ways of life and cultural knowledge as disappearing, as a result of the trauma and dislocation of 1948, the continued efforts of the Israeli government to de-Arabize and Judaize local culture, and a more generic process of urbanization. Because of the medium's distribution as pamphlets and because the purpose of the medium was cultural survival, oral history gave scholars the role of engaged intellectuals. Their work focused on refugees and rural ways of life, which were recurrent themes among artists, intellectuals, and publications of the Palestinian national movement.

Since 2000, oral history and ethnography shifted to focus on the experiences of young, urban, and working people. Young working women carved a niche for themselves in the oral history medium and in the discourse of sumud (steadfastness). In my work, I found that midwives were excellent users of oral history. They told long, sustained narratives of the self. They spoke of themselves as struggling and working gendered persons who were financially and psychologically independent. They saw themselves as different from their mother's generation and different from the men of their own generation because they were the main breadwinners. In fact, I tried to interview the husbands and brothers of midwives but they were uninterested. The closure and job market were gendered insofar as many men were less mobile and could not find employment. In this context, they did not feel that oral history would have value in their lives. On the other hand, the midwives in the oral histories presented a new desirable type of classed femininity. A woman from a poor background with an education and a low paid job who worked and struggled for decades could do well, be upwardly mobile, and live somewhat disengaged from male kin.

PART TWO

Sumud and the Infrastructure of Health

4

Work in Sumud Institutions and Its Situated Meanings

In the second part of the book, I shift from oral histories and birth stories to a focus on the institutions and infrastructures of birth. The story is spiraling outward from new mothers to midwives, to doctors and the infrastructure of birth. First, I will describe the large, urban, and charitable hospital funded for many years by sumud funds. Charitable institutions and social networks are particularly important in the Middle East.[1] Their historical significance has complicated scholarly theories of governmentality that focus on the relationship between subjects and the state. In the Occupied Territories, Jordan and then the PLO started rallying funds to support charitable institutions and businesses, which created a hierarchical infrastructure. This chapter will explore what it is like to work in sumud institutions. Doctors in sumud institutions were keen to tell the history of the birthing infrastructure, especially the history of the large, centralized hospitals where they were both medical practitioners and decision-makers. They thought of themselves as politically committed to the nationalist cause through their work. Given the discourse and funding from the PLO, doctors used the concept of *sumud* (steadfastness) to explain the culture, drive, and success of their institutions. I will show how birthing professionals expanded the meaning of sumud to describe and explain how they lived and worked in order to survive occupation. Nurses and midwives, however, challenged the success narrative to highlight

1. For work on charities, aid, and subjectivity in Palestine, see Feldman (2015, 2018); Fassin (2008).

exploitation and class difference. They reappropriated the word "sumud" to mean a type of classed work and politics they performed through everyday work, dealing with an increased case load and decreased staff, as well as the inability to visit their families often due to the closure. Every day, with small struggles, they pushed against the closure. For example, they used cell phone technology to assist with births when women were unable to reach Jerusalem and every day after their shifts, they called their children and families in an effort to keep their families together.

Sumud as a Type of Funding and Top-Down Policy

At the level of state or party politics, sumud is first and foremost the name of a financial development policy on the part of the PLO and Arab governments responding to Israel's 1967 occupation of the West Bank and Gaza Strip. Among the first policies implemented by the Israeli military government in 1967 was the closure of banking and financial services, eliminating sources of credit for Palestinian entrepreneurs (Sandler and Frisch 1984, 49). Likewise, hundreds of military orders impeded Palestinian industry and agriculture. Simultaneously, Israeli industry, agriculture, and construction expanded rapidly after 1967, creating jobs that Palestinian workers took as a result of their own enterprises' failing. From the viewpoint of Arab governments, it was a priority to construct what Yezid Sayigh has called parallel institutionalization (1997, 468), or an alternative system of social services and economic opportunities separate from Israeli state institutions.

Directly after the occupation of the West Bank, Jordan was the first to announce its policy of "sumud," which entailed refusing to participate in social, political, or administrative activities directed by the Israeli military authorities. They pledged to refrain from founding new institutions since that would involve registration under Israeli auspices. A famous episode of this policy was the Jordanian support for the striking Palestinian lawyers, judges, and teachers in the West Bank who refused to recognize the legitimacy of the Israeli-run administration. Jordan paid their salaries with financial support from the Arab League on and off from 1967 until 1988 (Sayigh 1997, 466). Through the funding of institutions such as unions, mayors' offices and individuals, the Jordanian government sought Palestinians' political allegiance in competition with the PLO. By the mid-1970s, Jordanian support through sumud continued and there was tacit cooperation between the Israeli Civil Administration and the Jordan-funded institutions in the Occupied Territories, which included unions, schools, orphanages, and hospitals (Sayigh 1997, 466; Sandler and Frish 1984, 47–48).

Between 1964, when the PLO was founded, and 1978, the PLO was not competing with Jordan over funding institutions in the Palestinian Occupied Territories. Rather, it focused its politics on military and civilian resistance, first from within Jordan, until the Jordanian government massacred and expelled them in September 1970. The PLO then relocated to Lebanon after the Cairo Accords, which authorized the PLO to continue its activities in Lebanon. As of the late 1970s, however, the PLO shifted its politics to supporting the parallel construction of an alternative system of social services and economic opportunities in Lebanon and the Palestinian Occupied Territories. In 1978, sumud sources of financial assistance expanded from Jordan to other Arab states and coincided with this shift in PLO politics.

Sumud funds were collected through a series of diplomatic alliances forged between Arab states under the aegis of the "steadfastness front." In November 1977, Egypt's president, Anwar Sadat, visited Jerusalem and began formal diplomatic relations with Israel, breaking Arab nations' refusal to enter into relations with Israel since the 1948 declaration of war and defeat of Arab armies. Egypt was the first Arab country to do so. In response, other Arab statesmen met at a summit in Baghdad and decided to reject Egypt's political line and instead fund what they called the steadfastness of Syria, Jordan, and Palestine to support the difficulties they would face by remaining against diplomatic relations with Israel. At a second summit in December of 1977 in Tripoli, Libya, Arab statesmen founded the "steadfastness and confrontation front" (*jabhat al ṣumūd wal taṣaḍi*), which included Libya, Algeria, Tunisia, South Yemen, the PLO, Syria, and Iraq (although it was not present at Tripoli because of its conflict with the Syrian Baath).[2] This front proposed three goals: (1) to reject Egypt's political line, (2) to unite the fractured Palestinian political groups under the umbrella organization of the PLO, and (3) to begin a Syrian-Iraqi rapprochement (Abu Shreef 2005, 69). The steadfastness and confrontation front dissolved in 1980–81 as a result of the worsening conflict between Syria and Iraq and Iraq's need to fund its war with Iran.[3] However, the idea of the "rejection camp" (*miḥwar almumāna'a*) remains in Arab political discourse to this day, although it has shifted its meaning to a newer allegiance between Iran, Syria, and the Lebanese Hizballah.[4]

The PLO leadership, especially Yasser Arafat and Khalil Al-Wazir, built alliances with various Arab governments to secure funds and temporary

2. Arab nationalism, born with the decline and fall of the Ottoman Empire, proclaimed the objective of uniting all of the (approximately twenty-two) Arab countries from the Atlantic Ocean to the Persian Gulf. One of its incarnations was the Baath Party (The Arab Socialist Baath Party), whose fundamental principles were proclaimed by a Syrian political thinker, Michel Aflaq. It attracted supporters in the Eastern Arab world, notably Syria and Iraq, as well as, to a lesser extent, Jordan, Lebanon, and Palestine. It was nondenominational and socialist. The Baath took power through a combination of elections and military coups in Iraq and Syria during the first half of the 1960s. In Syria, Baathist ideology became the means whereby non-Sunni politicians could hope to share in national power and wealth. Through their positions in the army, Alawites were able to seize power within the Baath Party and then the state, in which they have been hegemonic ever since, under Hafez al-Assad and his son Bashar.

3. Iraq under Saddam Hussein invaded Iran in 1980, following Khomeini's Islamic revolution, with the intention of overthrowing the new regime. Because of its supposed attraction for the majority Shia population of Iraq, Iran was considered an imminent threat to the power of Saddam and the Baath party. The war cost millions of casualties on both sides, and lasted eight years. Syria did not join the Arab consensus in support of Iraq and, on the contrary, carefully marked out areas of cooperation, principally economic, with the Islamic Republic. Although Assad's Syria never supported the Iranian-style Islamization of Iraq, the Saddam regime considered its position treasonous, during what it saw as the country's hour of greatest need. Shortly following the end of the Iraq-Iran War, Saddam invaded Kuwait in 1990 in the quest for additional oil revenues. In response, the United States gathered a coalition of states to free the country. Syria joined this coalition, thus adding to the contentious relations between the two countries.

4. See Moghnieh (2021) for an analysis of the way Hizballah and Lebanese public culture used sumud since the July 2006 war.

protection for the PLO in Arab countries. In 1977, the PLO, headed by Arafat, joined the "steadfastness and rejection" front, while at the same time negotiating unofficially with Sadat and US governments. This front reopened channels of negotiation with King Hussein of Jordan, which had been cut after Black September and the eviction of the PLO leadership from Jordan in 1970–71 (Abu Rish 1998; Abu Shreef 2005; Sayigh 1997).[5] Through savvy diplomacy, the PLO reaped the financial benefits of multiple sumud funders, including Jordan, the Steadfastness and Rejection Front (mainly from the oil producing economies of Libya and Algeria), and private Palestinian businessmen in Kuwait, Saudi Arabia, and Jordan.

Access to funding consolidated the power of Yasser Arafat and assured him further patronage from segments of Palestinian society (Sayigh 1997, 458). In Lebanon during the years of the revolution (1971–82), the process of patronage, known as *tafrīgh*, placed a substantial proportion of Palestinian refugees on the payroll (Sayigh 1997, 459). *Tafrīgh* was extended not only to the militia but also to PLO civilian organizations such as student unions, worker unions, and women's organizations. In addition to a basic salary (the lowest among the Lebanese guerrilla groups but still significant), Fatah members were entitled to a wedding allowance, cost-of-living allowances, and social security.[6] This type of patronage consolidated the

---

5. The PLO, founded in 1964, was at first considered a useful tool of the major Arab countries. Until the defeat of June 1967 at the hands of Israel, Jordan saw little reason to curtail the organization's recruitment campaigns, centered in the refugee camps. This changed progressively, beginning with the highly symbolic battle of Karameh in 1968, in which irregular PLO forces led by Yasser Arafat and supported by Jordanian artillery, repulsed the Israeli attack on the Karameh military base. Buoyed by this feat, thousands of young people flocked to one or another of the PLO factions, mainly Arafat's Fatah group, enlisting as *fidayīn* (guerrilla fighters) in the cause of freedom and self-determination. From that moment on, the Palestinian presence in Jordan became an existential threat for King Hussein and the Jordanian-Bedouin establishment. King Hussein finally responded with a concerted military campaign beginning in September 1970 and lasting until the following summer, through which PLO members, armed and administrative, were driven out of the country. Most of them regrouped in Lebanon.

6. "Fatah" is the acronym for the Arabic *ḥarakat al-taḥrīr al-waṭani al-filastīnī* (the Palestinian National Liberation Movement). Founded in 1959 by a group around Yasser

power of Yasser Arafat and others in PLO leadership roles, as well as constructed dependent institutions (Sayigh 1997). It also transformed Palestinian members of militias and organizations "from unpaid volunteers to petty salariat" (Sayigh 1997, 461). In Palestine, the PLO emphasized sumud by providing services and public goods, allocating a total of $463 million in funds by the end of 1986, which accounted for one third of all external transfers to the Occupied Territories, excluding the United Nations Relief and Works Agency (UNRWA) expenditures (612). Through its funding of what Joost Hilterman (1991) called "hierarchical paternalistic charitable organizations," sumud funds strengthened the hand of Palestinian entrepreneurs and managers of institutions, but complicated the work of trade unions and workers.

The diplomatic efforts of the PLO and the relationships it created with people through its funding of party members and social services is an important part of the story and affects the cultures and functioning of sumud institutions. But what we have heard less about is what it is like to work in a sumud institution. The doctors and nurses in Makassed hospital rejected the idea that they had been coopted by funding for social services, although they were well aware of their dependence on it. They often said that they were actively redefining what sumud meant. For doctors, this entailed working to make things functioned despite occupation. And for

---

Arafat, it was the first with a specifically Palestinian, rather than pan-Arab focus. When the principal Arab states were easily defeated by Israel in June 1967, it rose steadily, becoming the central party in the umbrella grouping, the Palestine Liberation Organization (PLO), Arafat heading both Fatah and the PLO from 1968 to his death in 2004. It led the largely ineffective guerrilla campaign to regain Palestine from 1968 to 1982 departing from Jordanian, then Lebanese bases, until Israel invaded Lebanon in 1982 and expelled the Palestinian fighters. From then on, it concentrated on political (and occasional military) resistance in the occupied West Bank and Gaza, until the Oslo Accords of 1993 brought it into the newly created Palestinian Authority (PA), charged with exercising limited self-government under overall Israeli sovereignty. The head of Fatah became the chairman of the PA in addition to the PLO, and this arrangement continued under Arafat's successor, Mahmoud Abbas. Its past as a liberation movement still permeates Fatah's discourse, but not its practice, which has become largely bureaucratized.

nurses it entailed work and efforts in patient care and came with exploitation and class differences. In the following sections, I will explore these experiences and what it is like to work in sumud institutions.

Charitable Institutions and Social Networks in the Middle East

As mentioned above, the sumud (steadfastness) infrastructure took shape in the period between the 1967 Israeli occupation of the West Bank and Gaza and the outbreak of the First Intifada (uprising) in December 1987. During my time in the field, I worked at a charitable hospital, a specific type of sumud institution. Makassed Hospital in East Jerusalem represents an urban, technological model of care, which is part of the public health sector that was built during a movement that contributed infrastructure to occupied Palestinian territories, including the West Bank, East Jerusalem, and the Gaza Strip. Viewing Palestinian society through the lens of medical institutions and a charitable institution, in particular, has a number of advantages. First, medicine is an important institution in the history of modern nation building in the Middle East (Hamdy 2012; Dewachi 2017). Second, hospitals and clinics were one of the first sites of employment for women at the turn of the century and, along with schools, remain important employers for women. Finally, medical professions are varied in terms of class and regional belonging, which gave me access to different segments of society (including upper-middle-class urbanized men and women, middle-class rural families, working-class rural women, and refugee women).

Hospitals were an obvious research site because 98 percent of births take place in hospitals. Likewise, when I started working in hospitals, I found that employees and people, in general, often spoke about social and medical movements such as "sumud" and the "popular health movement" as central to constructing cultures of birth and medicine. I had expected to be confronted more directly with state practices (be it those of the occupation or of the Palestinian Authority [PA]) and the formation of individual subjectivities. Instead, I was struck by the importance people attached to social movements. It is for this reason that I begin by engaging with the particular set of social movements and healthcare.

Literature on health institutions has focused on the ways in which medical practices and discourses produce different regimes of health and control. Michel Foucault is the paramount influence for shaping the understanding of how biology, medicine, and governance interact. Foucault's (2004) concept of governmentality designates a distinctly modern form of rule that aims to govern more efficiently by rendering individuals capable of augmenting their own welfare. It has three interrelated elements: government or the management of population; discipline, which concerns practices and techniques of rule; and sovereignty—that is, territory and laws. Building on Foucault's formulation of biopower and focusing on the third of these elements, Giorgio Agamben (1998) links the amalgamation of sovereign and medical power in Europe to the "biologized" notion of rights that emerged at the time of the French Revolution. He argues that, with the postrevolutionary body becoming the site of rights from the moment of birth—that is, when the body became the ground of sovereign subjects—the sovereign is partially displaced by another figure, the doctor, the one responsible for the care of the body.

In his PhD dissertation on doctors and sovereignty in Syria from the mid-nineteenth to the early twentieth century, Robert Blecher (2002) shows that in the Middle East, the notion of individual rights has a different genealogy specific to the region's history. He demonstrates that Ottoman governmentality differed from its European equivalent insofar as it departed from the fixation on the individual. The European state appeared to retract itself from certain realms to create seemingly "emancipated zones" where individual rights were articulated through civil society. In the Ottoman Levant, by contrast, which included greater Syria, Blecher identifies the new "social networks" of the early twentieth century as crucial units with historical importance. These urban, civic, gender-based, national, and professional groups of social actors, while tied to the state, remained autonomous. Despite this difference in focus, European governmentality, like its Ottoman counterpart, was mainly designed to protect the interests of the population. In the colonial context, on the other hand, European states used techniques of governmentality as tools of coercion in ways that violated metropolitan norms. Ottoman and post-Ottoman societies thus differ from both Western and colonial models by placing autonomous networks of social agents at the center. This insight suggests the need to view the Palestinian case (and others) in a particular light that differs from standard academic treatment.

Since Ernest Renan ([1882] 1998, 32) and, more recently, Benedict Anderson (1991), the structural relationship that establishes the national entity has been seen as that which links the individual and the state, passing through the workings of print capitalism.[7] While this triangle is relevant, I suggest that in post-Ottoman societies, other dimensions need to be taken into consideration. For example, in Ottoman contexts, professional corporations emerged from social settings where, historically, nation building was not on the agenda. The historiography of the Arab East points overwhelmingly to continued loyalty to the Ottoman state until the outbreak of World War I. Therefore, and although we are dealing with a simultaneously colonial and postcolonial context in Palestine, specific and deeply entrenched sociopolitical elements have carried over from an earlier period in the medical sphere, among others.

Arguably the most important body of work on colonial and postcolonial subjects has been carried out by the Subaltern Studies Group—whose historians have sought to recover subaltern subjectivity from the various epistemologies that have erased it (Spivak 1988). Building on Foucault's concepts, they pay close attention to the relationship between the state and the subaltern in India (Guha and Spivak 1988) and, in the process, establish a model with many applications. In this spirit, Blecher shows that in the Middle East, networks and groups of individuals having similar characteristics (professional, charitable, civic, gender-based) need to be understood collectively as an additional actor, not encompassed within the colonial and anticolonial dialectic and, therefore, as a unit of analysis endowed with historical agency. It is with this specific analytical

7. Rashid Khalidi provides further support for this view when, in *Palestinian Identity* (1997), he illustrates the progressive construction of the nation through the proliferation of events from the eighteenth century onward, as depicted, in particular, by the Palestinian press.

configuration in mind (neither metropolitan nor colonial) that the present chapter explores the slow process whereby deeply rooted affinity groups and networks became an essential element of the still ongoing state and nation-building process. In light of these perspectives, I show that the medical professions and institutions that support them are deeply intertwined with political authority.[8]

The two movements in the history of Palestinian public health recounted here, sumud, and in the following chapter, popular health, were the focus of many discussions about health care. Stories from Jerusalem, the capital, and the hospital focused on the concept of sumud. Those from Ramallah, other parts of Palestine, and the clinic related more closely to the popular health movement. Looming in the background are two contrasting but related projections of the nation. The first is embedded in stories about the medical infrastructure and birth, as represented by Makassed Hospital in Jerusalem, the Palestinian hospital par excellence. The hospital can be viewed as an analog to the successful nation, with its competent leader and spokesperson, the doctor; its hardworking, sacrificing citizens, the nurse, midwife, and technician; and its modern organization, sophisticated technology, successful operation, clean building, and transparent financing. The envisioned nation here is a centralized one in which the political elites are chosen by the people and reflect the general will. It is also a positivist vision of the nation in which technology provides the means for solving social problems.

The second projection of the nation was concerned with the popular health movement and the Union of Palestinian Medical Relief Committees (UPRMC) and its afterlives and presents an alternate microcosm, based on a social-formations concept in which the Palestinian nation cannot be divorced from society and its component parts. The health professionals in the popular health movement strove to extend the benefits of primary healthcare from the single institution of the hospital to the villages, camps, and towns of Palestine in the form of clinics. This socially

---

8. See Hamdy (2012); Dewachi (2017); and Hamdy and Bayoumi (2016) for an analysis of the ways medical and political authority are connected.

based vision of the nation incorporates lessons from the socialist model, not as it was, but as it was envisioned to be practiced. Implicit in this artic- ulation of the nation through an alternative health system is the effort to save the socialist model by radically restructuring it. As will be seen, both visions engendered internal dissent and, in the end, both adopted verti- cal and paternalistic forms of operation. Furthermore, both visions of the nation and accompanying visions of a health care system suggest that the two types of politics of health have in common a historically rooted form of charitable institution that played an important role in the making of modern subjectivities in the Middle East.

Sumud at Makassed Hospital in Jerusalem

Makassed sits on the Mount of Olives in Jerusalem. It has a capacity of 250 beds, which amounts to roughly 45 percent of the total hospital beds in East Jerusalem, and is staffed by 560 employees. It has nine departments of medicine and its department of obstetrics and gynecology is known throughout Palestine. In addition to normal and high-risk obstetric care, it provides gynecological surgery and has a well-known infertility and perinatology clinic. It is the main teaching hospital for doctors, special- ists, midwives, and nurses. It is affiliated with the first Palestinian medi- cal school, established in 1994 at Al-Quds University. Prior to that time, all medical students were obliged to study and train outside the country. Since 1988, Makassed has also provided a four-year specialization pro- gram in obstetrics, where general practitioners train to be obstetricians and pass the Jordanian Board Certification exam.

Until the 1990s, Makassed received patients from all over the Occu- pied Territories. However, with the tight closure of Jerusalem in 2000, most Palestinians from the West Bank no longer have access and it mainly serves Palestinians from the immediate area. Since it is a nongovernmen- tal, albeit charitable, hospital, the cost of treatment is cheaper than equiva- lent services in the private sector. However, it is considerably higher than at government institutions, which have been free of charge for childbirth services since the outbreak of the Second Intifada. In addition, Makassed offers reduced costs according to household income. Upper-middle-class people, as well as poorer people, obtain treatment there. With its impressive technologies, interest in medical education, diverse clientele, and universalist aspirations, it is a working symbol of the Palestinian national movement's dreams.

In the early days of my research, I spoke with Dr. Rami, a prominent obstetrician at Makassed. When I asked what Makassed Hospital was like, he described its history as intimately linked with that of sumud. The sumud policy of the PLO promoted a type of nonviolent resistance whereby Palestinians under occupation received material support from external sources as they endured difficult military and political measures and a harsh economic situation for the sake of their national future. The PLO and Arab governments sent funds to support local industries and services to sustain living conditions in the Occupied Territories. This was a response and challenge to the poor government services offered by the Israeli military's "civil administration," which controlled governmental, health, and educational institutions.[9] The sumud approach was rooted in Arab and Palestinian nationalism, which understood colonialism and military rule to be the major cause of poverty and obstacle to development. Sumud-linked donations were supposed to alleviate poverty and encourage Palestinians to stay put. In 1978 Arab leaders officially started the pan-Arab fund, *amwāl al-ṣumūd*, to be administered jointly by Jordan and the PLO, and which called on Palestinians in the Occupied Territories to be *ṣamidīn* (steadfast).

When discussing the genealogy of funding sources, which is well-known throughout the country but has few records due to the illegal status of the PLO prior to 1993, Dr. Rami and other physicians signaled the institution's connection to sumud, a source of local prestige. Through the sumud fund, the Arab states believed they were infusing the country with

---

9. Between 1967 and 1994, the Palestinian health system was under the control of Israel's defense ministry, with the officer for health playing the role of minister. At public institutions, his prerogatives included the payment of salaries and the hiring and firing of Palestinian medical personnel, as well as the setting of health policies. The actual health providers were Palestinians.

the means to survive, while different forms of resistance would hasten the demise of the occupation. Like the PLO itself, and in keeping with the ebb and flow of international politics, the hospital saw a succession of donors. With its leadership and departments, Makassed reflected an ideal state institution. However, in this case, the PLO was not a sovereign state actor and it was illegal to have any connection with it, financial or otherwise. Nonetheless, Makassed was one of the Palestinian hospitals considered financially stable. And while it had large debts, Dr. Rami explained that it managed to cover salaries every month through received donations (another demonstration of sumud). That said, at the time of our initial encounter in 2002, employees of the hospital had not received salaries for a few months. According to Dr. Rami, this was a problem of liquidity, based simply on delays caused by Israel and the Palestinian Authority in clearing the donations and passing them on to the hospital.

The institution's continued limited resources and liquidity problems suggested that it was not as financially stable as some portrayed it to be. It did continue to pay salaries, even if late in coming, something very few large institutions, such as the universities, could claim (World Bank 2003, 45). Despite the liquidity and funding problems, people talked about Makassed as a strong, resilient, and stable institution. It maintained that image of strength, not only because in the end finances were covered, but also because it has a symbolic and historical connection to the Palestinian national movement. Unlike the private hospitals, which started sprouting up in the mid-1990s and were subject to the whims of economic and political changes, Makassed appeared to have the stability of a national infrastructure. In fact, while it had managed to stay afloat over the years, the multiple changes in sources of funding illustrates the unstable political conditions with which Palestinian institutions had to cope. Describing the source of sumud funds, Dr. Rami noted: "It has been funded regularly since its beginnings in 1968. Before the Gulf War, most of the funding came from Kuwait and Saudi Arabia. After 1991, it had to depend more on other Gulf countries like the United Arab Emirates and Qatar." Since the Palestinian leadership sided against the United States and its allies during the Gulf War, Kuwait and Saudi Arabia took away their funding. But other Gulf countries replaced them. Makassed managed to weather the 1991 Gulf War and had sufficient donations through the 1993–2000 Oslo period, thanks to sumud funds.[10]

A majority of nationalists, for some time prior to Oslo, had espoused the politics of sumud across political and professional sectors. According to the ideology of the time, real and lasting solutions to health problems could only be achieved with a just and durable resolution of the political crisis. In the meantime, however, the development of a Palestinian infrastructure within the limits imposed by Israeli military laws and practices was the aim. Palestinian administrators agreed to fight for permits and licenses in the offices of the Israeli military governor for the renewal or inception of each project. Some applications were denied, others granted. But an inherent principle of the politics of sumud was to act openly and with the toleration of the military governor; department after department was created and staffed. Leaders and activists set up the basic infrastructure of Palestinian curative services in the Occupied Territories. They bought medical technologies and developed expertise. Other Palestinian hospitals were large, bureaucratic, and located in urban areas, and while they aspired to sophisticated technologies and specialized services, most did not possess the means for them. Makassed was "as good and advanced as Israeli hospitals," Dr. Rami said with pride.

10. The series of agreements between Israel and the PLO, beginning in September 1993 with the *Declaration of Principles*, and continuing with the Paris economic protocols (1994) and the Taba agreement (1995), together make up the Oslo Accords, by which the "Oslo" or "interim" phase of Palestinian history was inaugurated. In this transitional phase, the newly established Palestinian Authority (consisting of a presidency and a legislative council) would assume responsibility for the affairs of the area under its responsibility (parts of the West Bank and much of the Gaza Strip). Israel committed to a phased withdrawal over a five-year period, following which a final settlement would be agreed. For the Palestinians and under international law, this of necessity meant national self-determination and, given the overwhelming will of Palestinians, the creation of a state in the totality of the territories occupied by Israel in June 1967. It would appear that the Israeli leadership never saw things in this light—in a sense, the interim phase was to be the final one.

Being a sumud dependent institution meant there was fluctuation in funding sources: from notables and clubs in Jerusalem and Beirut to the Jordanian state, Kuwait, and the UAE. And at each turn in PLO diplomacy, the hospital has been under threat of shutting down, oftentimes being late paying salaries, but after negotiations and political maneuvering, it manages to find different sources of funding. And the changing diplomacy and unstable sources of funding affect the work of managers and employees of sumud institutions. In a way, sumud as ideology obligates Arab nations to give. The failure of a flagship sumud institution such as Makassed would be viewed as shameful and a failure for all Arab nations. Makassed therefore does not merely have the support of continued funding but also the stability of an entrenched ideology that drives the funding.

Practices of Sumud

This same genealogy of instability and severing of diplomatic ties is also a source of pride that gives meaning to employees' work. Arab leaders gave the concept of sumud a prominent place in political discourse regarding Palestine, even as Palestinians in the Occupied Territories were reading new meanings into it, insisting on the fact that sumud is a lived experience and practice, thus carving a niche for themselves in official politics. Palestinians in the territories and in Israel had been speaking of sumud as a form of daily political action since the 1950s, before Arab governments and the PLO began their politics of sumud funds. The purpose of such discourse was to empower them to endure clinging to their homes, their lands, and their activities. In his published journal *The Third Way*, Raja Shehadeh (1982, viii), author and human rights lawyer, writes of the everyday practices of sumud:

> Long before Arab politicians outside defined sumud as a pan-Arab objective, it had been practiced by every man, woman and child here struggling on his or her own to learn to cope with, and resist, the pressures of living as a member of a conquered people. Sumud is watching your home turned into a prison. You, Samid, choose to stay in that prison, because it is your home, and because you fear that if you leave,

your jailer will not allow you to return. Living like this, you must constantly resist the twin temptations of either acquiescing in the jailer's plan in numb despair, or becoming crazed by consuming hatred for your jailer and yourself, the prisoner. It is from this personal basis that sumud for us, in contrast with politicians outside, is developing from an all-encompassing form of life into a form of resistance that unites the Palestinians living under Israeli occupation.

In this quote, Shehadeh describes a different kind of sumud, one that is practiced every day by people living under occupation. He likens the experience of sumud to the life of prisoners and focuses on lived experiences and emotions, in contrast to the discourse of sumud taken up by the PLO and Arab governments in the diaspora. This was not the first or last time that the people had carved a niche for themselves in the Arab discourse of sumud to give value to their everyday work. In her ethnography of gender during the Palestinian "revolution years" (1975–82) in Lebanon, Julie Peteet (1991) documents how Palestinian camp women appropriated the term to talk about and give value to the housework and child-rearing they were doing at home.

In her more recent analysis of the semantics of psychological experiences in Lebanon, Lamia Moghnieh (2021) analyzes the connections of sumud to trauma in public discourse. She explains the ways the meanings of words shifted. Sumud was the binary opposite of trauma during the July war in 2006, contributing to the bewilderment of the psychiatric community, who had trouble finding pathological traces of war events on people in Lebanon. Starting with the Syrian refugee crisis in 2011, "trauma portfolios" began to emerge (James 2004, 131), documenting and recognizing persons as victims and survivors of violence. This corresponded with the gradual fading of sumud's evocative power.

In Palestine, Lena Meari argues that sumud embodies "a radical alterity to the conceptions, sensibilities, attachments, and practices of humanitarian psychiatry" (2014b, 77). She documents how political activists, who are members of the Palestinian Front for the Liberation of Palestine (PFLP), as well as former prisoners of the late 1970s through the 1980s, use the concept of sumud as a process of imagination to survive torture and interrogation (2014b).[11] After their release, they consciously cultivated the concept in Palestinian society and reorganized familial and social relations. Meari presents moments from everyday life where sumud is visibly part of intimate relationships, such as the scene of a mother sending a note with a lawyer to tell her son under interrogation that "your mom says she prefers to hear the news of your death than of confession" (558).[12] For many people like Dr. Rami in Palestine, sumud is practiced in everyday life. He understood his efforts and that of his colleagues, defying restrictions on mobility to reach the workplace and dealing with the discontinuity of care due to the closure, as part of that work of perseverance.

While Makassed always had patients, it was difficult for doctors to anticipate where they would come from and whether there would be an avalanche or a dearth thereof. Since the beginning of the prolonged closure in the early 1990s, patients from the Gaza Strip were rare because they were not given permits to travel. But patient numbers from the West Bank also fluctuated. The first phase of closure targeted Jerusalem; as a result, patients started going to hospitals in other towns. After Ramallah was reoccupied by the Israeli military in 2002, those who could returned to Jerusalem. People living in surrounding villages such as Hizma, Anata, and Abu Dis, and some in the Ramallah and Bethlehem areas, found it easier to get to Jerusalem than to the nearest town. Everything seemed to depend on the constellation of the closure, "We always have patients, but the question is from where and how many?" Dr. Rami continued:

> My patient from Ras Karkar [a village close to Ramallah], she comes here like many because she has high-risk pregnancies. She had two previous cesareans and suffers from diabetes. She thought it would be easier

---

11. The Popular Front for the Liberation of Palestine (PFLP) is a Marxist-Leninist and revolutionary socialist organization founded in 1967 by George Habash. The PFLP has generally taken a hard line on Palestinian national aspirations, opposing the more moderate stance of Fatah. It opposes negotiations with the Israeli government and states that it is fighting for a state on the whole of 1948 Palestine.

12. See also the work of Ismail Nashef (2008) on the concept of sumud among Palestinian prisoners.

to drive 40 km to Jerusalem than get to Ramallah. We set up an appointment for the C-section, but she was unable to cross the checkpoint that day. She arrived knocking at my door four days later, and I had to stop everything, because her case was getting dangerous.

My ongoing observations indicate that this was the precarious way in which medical care was dispensed and births assisted in Palestinian hospitals. The medical practices learned as routine were no longer viable in this unpredictable situation. Only rarely did medical providers see a woman prior to her arrival, already in labor, at which point they barely had time to gain the necessary patient background information. Working for and managing a hospital under such conditions was experienced as part of the lived politics of sumud. Employees could never be certain they would reach the hospital. For example, a resident in the anesthesia department, whom Dr. Rami drove to and from Ramallah, first had to take a five-hour drive from Tulkarem. And Dr. Rami himself was not much better off: "For two weeks I could not come to work. A doctor here took my place during that time. But it is still a mess. And can you imagine the road every day?" It was difficult to know who would come to work and who wouldn't, which patient would arrive and which one wouldn't; nonetheless, the hospital continued to function and adapt.

I could imagine it, in fact, because during this phase of my fieldwork, I often traveled the same road Dr. Rami took every day and collected many of my own stories of waiting, standing in line, delays, frustration, and not understanding the logic. Passing Qalandia, the main checkpoint between Ramallah and Jerusalem, had been a strenuous and lengthy affair since the spring of 2001. Pedestrians—whether peasants, workers, doctors, lawyers, or butchers—all lined up in the dust of a rundown road to get their IDs checked by a soldier. The alternative was to take a longer roundabout road where people, especially men, ran the risk of being arrested. Most therefore went through the Qalandia checkpoint. Things worsened with the beginning of the construction of the wall when unofficial roads (al-turuq al-sha'biyya, or peoples' roads, as they are known) were progressively choked off, and the turnstiles modernized. The waiting was the same, the frustration perhaps greater (because of dwindling options) and the noise and dust pollution levels still very high. Closure stories have become a communal account that refugees, returnees, urban and rural people, men and women, poor and wealthy all share.[13] This is not to say that the effects of the closure are equal for all Palestinians regardless of class. However, the politics of the closure, the delays, standing in line, surveillance, being refused entry, and being under curfew in your home, as well as breaking the closure regulation, bypassing the checkpoint on winding dirt roads, or slipping out after sunset during curfew days, are told and retold as a communal story of a whole people, especially when the destination is the hospital, which symbolizes a lifeline of the nation.

Beginnings

The very creation of Makassed Hospital represented a victory for the Palestinian national movement and is emblematic of remaining steadfast. "There are two events in the hospital's history that single it out as the most important hospital in the Occupied Territories," Dr. Rami remarked. In 1964 the Al-Makassed Foundation started building a hospital on the Mount of Olives in Jerusalem. In 1967, when Israel occupied the West Bank and Gaza, the hospital was being built on land owned by the Islamic *awqāf* (religious endowment fund). Right after the occupation of Jerusalem, the Israeli army decided to expropriate the still empty hospital building and transform it into a police station. Hundreds of doctors and nurses mobilized. They moved beds, equipment, and even patients from private clinics and homes into Makassed premises and stayed in the hospital until Israeli authorities gave up control of the building.[14] The Makassed Foundation had just finished building the hospital at the time of the occupation. Filling the building with beds and equipment, doctors and nurses unofficially inaugurated the hospital at the beginning of occupation, which took on foundational importance. The official inauguration was not until 1968,

13. The term "returnees" designates Palestinians from the diaspora, usually belonging to the PLO in exile, who came to the Occupied Territories with Yasser Arafat in 1994 or thereafter.

14. For another account of these events, see Barghouti and Giacaman (1990).

but its initial movement against occupation, according to Dr. Rami, made a name for Makassed right from the start.

Then the 1987 intifada secured the hospital's position as an emblem of Palestinian nationalism. By early 1988, government hospitals, controlled by the Israeli so-called Civil Administration, under the aegis of the Ministry of Defense, were inundated with injured persons. Their services were not sufficient; as a result, the injured from all over the Occupied Territories, from Gaza in the south to Jenin in the north, flocked to Makassed. There were no checkpoints at that time and the roads were easy. Furthermore, the hospital specializes in high-tech, complicated, emergency surgery. And, like many other hospitals, intifada injuries were treated free of charge. Makassed became the most prominent Palestinian hospital.

The hospital's foundation story in 1967 resembles popular stories about what happened to the entire country when it came under occupation. It is a story about waking up to the necessity of joining the struggle, an impulsive awakening. It is the year the PLO opted for Fatah's historical insistence of steering clear of Arab nationalism of any stripe and concentrating on the Palestinian project. The decisive victory of the Palestinians over the Arab nationalist program resulted from the battle of Karameh in March 1968, in which Israeli forces withdrew after an onslaught onto a Fatah military camp in Jordan, suffering relatively heavy casualties. Yasir Arafat had, personally and against the advice of many of his peers, insisted on standing firm rather than opting for a tactical withdrawal. For the Palestinians and other Arabs, the battle of Karameh was the beginning of a comeback after the humiliating defeat of the Six-Day War in June 1967 (Sayigh 1997), which is typically narrated as the quintessential story of loss, followed by an awakening, and then civil disobedience. Furthermore, since the sit-in in Makassed was carried out by the Palestinians under occupation and without resort to arms, it is part of the history of the everyday practices of sumud.

The late Palestinian author Ghassan Kanafani was the first to write about the psychological and political effects of 1967 in his novel *Returning to Haifa* (1969). It centers around the main character Said S., who is originally from Haifa but now a refugee in Ramallah. He lives comfortably in a nice house, forbids his children to become fighters, and waits for the day he can return to the home he was expelled from in 1948. In the rush to flee Haifa in 1948, this man and his wife were unable to take their first child with them. Suddenly, nineteen years later, when Israel occupied the West Bank, Said S. had the opportunity to travel to Israel, visit the house, and inquire about his firstborn, Khaled. In the house, he found an Israeli couple living with their twenty-year-old son, Dov. The couple had found Khaled/Dov and adopted him. The son was now an Israeli, served in the army, and wanted nothing to do with his Arab or Palestinian identity. On his car drive back to Ramallah, Said realizes that he must renounce even blood ties for the sake of the cause and wishes that his other son had joined the resistance. Kanafani's novel is about a middle-aged man's return to his town of origin after the 1967 occupation opened the borders between the West Bank and Israel and his awakening to the need to struggle.[15]

Makassed's foundation story of 1967 is also about an awakening and the impulse to join the struggle against occupation. The doctors and nurses joined the resistance by bringing their equipment and sitting in on the hospital grounds. Makassed is here a microcosm of the imagined nation-state.

The Midwife: Rebellious Intermediary

As I was chatting with the midwives in the nurses' room, a young midwife named Ruba walked in, singing and waving her purse. She took off her veil, tied her hair up, wiped the sweat off her face, and said: "The service taxi took the Tora Bora road, but we have our salaries!" Tora Bora designates a mountainous, winding dirt road people took to avoid checkpoints. It is, of course, a reference to the Tora Bora caves in Afghanistan, where the US Army was searching for Bin Laden. Seven Makassed midwives had sent Ruba to the Bank of Palestine in Ramallah to pick up their salaries. "The heat, the sweat, and the wait at Qalandia checkpoint on the way to Ramallah! That was something," Ruba said. "And the return was through the stone quarries."

15. For a discussion of Kanafani in the culture of Palestinian resistance, see Harlow (1996).

In interviews and discussions with midwives, they wanted to make sure that their working conditions would be part of the story I would write. From their perspective, the hospital is far from being the ideal nation and the doctor far from being the competent leader and spokesperson. One midwife told me that if I wanted to learn about childbirth in this hospital, I needed to know how many hours they worked per week, how much money they made, and how often they got to see their families. Through telling their own version of the childbirth story, they adjusted the version they correctly presumed I was told by the doctor a few days earlier. Samia explained to me:

> Makassed is late in paying its employees. It has happened before. But this time we have not been paid for three months. It is the longest time without pay I can remember. Today, they paid us. We get more or less 1000 NIS [New Israeli Shekels; about $250] per month. So they should not do this to us. We cannot afford to wait three months for our wages. We have bills to pay and children to raise. This makes it impossible for us to live regular and stable lives.

According to Samia and Ruba, the reason midwives at Makassed had been overworked since the beginning of the Second Intifada was that the number of births had increased. Midwives assist all "normal" vaginal births at most hospitals in the Occupied Territories. Hence, more births in their hospital meant more work for them. "We midwives [at Makassed] usually deliver two hundred babies per month. But since the closure we have been delivering three hundred. Since the tough closure on Ramallah and Bethlehem, it has become easier to come all the way to Jerusalem from neighboring villages than to go to a neighboring town." Samia gave an additional explanation for the rise in births at Makassed: "Palestinians from Jerusalem are now afraid to go to Jewish hospitals. Many people with blue [Jerusalem] IDs used to deliver in Hadassah or other Israeli hospitals.[16]

16. Palestinians from Jerusalem have blue identification cards, like Israelis and Palestinians born within the pre-1967 borders of Israel. Palestinians from the Occupied Territories (excluding Jerusalem) hold orange or green IDs. The difference in the color of the

But many women now tell me they don't want to go there. There are rumors that Arabs receive different treatment than Jews." Ruba talked about the same suspicions: "Because of the political situation, [Palestinian] women from Jerusalem are now afraid to go to Israeli hospitals. They say, "You don't know what they will do to me. Will they take revenge on me or my newborn? We don't know how we'll be treated." These stories were specific to the residents of Jerusalem, where women could choose to go to hospitals across the "Green Line" into West Jerusalem.[17] In fact, the increase in hospital births in 2002 was specific to the city of Jerusalem. In other West Bank cities, such as Ramallah, staff at some hospitals spoke of a radical decrease in the number of births, even of empty labor rooms during the curfews.

In addition to an increase in the number of births, the labor room at Makassed had fewer staff. There were usually sixteen midwives, but two had recently resigned. "With so few midwives and so many births, we can no longer work the way we used to. Now we cannot attend to many of the important aspects of midwifery care," Ruba said. Sometimes, they didn't have time to shower women after delivery or to show them how to breastfeed. They went on rounds from one woman to the next, doing no more than the basic medical checkup. Their stories about the closure intersected with those of the doctors. However, unlike doctors, midwives saw working conditions as the most important feature of their professional existence. They take pride in assisting births in contrast with the doctor, who "walks in the delivery room when the work is all over" (communication with a midwife at another hospital). They identified the doctor as a privileged elite whose self-ascribed role is based on the labor of others. It was important for the midwives to emphasize that the hospital was not the ideal entity it presented itself to be. All was not organized, rational, and smoothly productive. Sumud was a recurring theme among midwives, too,

---

Israeli ID cards is in itself a statement about which future nation Jerusalem should belong to (with, or for, the occupier, preferably without its blue ID-holding Palestinians). See Tawil-Souri (2011, 2012) for an analysis of IDs and their history and function in Palestinian society.

17. Green Line: the borders of Israel prior to the occupation of 1967.

but it had a social and subaltern slant. They too felt that their steadfastness was directed toward the political predicament, which the occupation, in general, and the system of closures, in particular, had placed them in. But they also felt that sumud was their continued work even in the face of poor conditions, for which the Palestinian employer was responsible. This form of sumud paralleled the combined national and social objectives of the 2000 intifada, directed as it was against the occupation and against a ruling elite by whom they felt exploited (Heacock 2008).

Another difference midwives pointed to between their profession and that of doctors was their closeness to a Palestinian social base and women's apparent preference for female birth attendants. Describing her previous job in Ramallah, Samia explained how mothers demanded that midwives rather than obstetricians assist their births. Opening in the mid-1990s, the hospital in question was part of the expanding private sector that emerged amid the hopes of looming peace and a rising economy. It vaunted its specialized, personalized, and luxurious services, targeting women who could afford the fees. The novelty of this maternity hospital was that obstetricians assisted normal births instead of midwives. According to Samia, midwives were dissatisfied with their secondary role despite the good salary, as they could not provide midwifery care according to their vision of the profession.[18] She decided to leave and go to Makassed. However, this Ramallah hospital was soon forced to change its policy due to a lack of clientele and permitted midwives to attend normal births upon a woman's request. Her story points to a main argument midwives continue to make to the ministry of health: unlike doctors' assistance at births, their work and presence at births is grounded in popular demand.

These stories reflect an increasingly visible tension between obstetricians and midwives in Palestine. As is the case in many other parts of the world, the professions of midwifery and obstetrics compete for the production of authoritative knowledge on childbirth (Davis-Floyd and Sargent 1997) and for the financial gain and markets that laboring women

18. According to the Palestinian Association of Obstetricians/Gynecologists, less than 10 percent of obstetricians working in West Bank hospitals are women.

represent. However, in contrast to other Arab countries in the Middle East (Egypt, Lebanon, and Jordan, for example), midwives in the West Bank assist almost all complication-free hospital births.[19] While they do not have their own union (they belong to the nurses' union, headed by a male nurse) and are relatively low in the hierarchy of the hospital staff, they exercise a certain power in Palestine because of the shortage of midwives and their popularity with patients.

Measures taken against the intifada, such as closures and curfews, disrupted the previous medical routine and organization of childbirth, which opened a space for different groups to restructure it. It was not surprising to hear discussions about the intensified rivalry between midwives and obstetricians. A midwife in a government hospital said that I could witness "the age-old fight between midwives and obstetricians here," as she drew an obstetrician who was walking by into the conversation. "They blame us for everything that goes wrong," she said, "and we tell them, 'You can start talking when you start doing the work.' We do all the births. Even with complicated births, we stay with the woman until she is fully dilated. Then, at the very end, the doctor comes in." The obstetrician retorted that doctors have other responsibilities, such as operative deliveries, outpatient cases, and gynecology cases. In another interview, an obstetrician exclaimed, while he was explaining the division of labor: "Midwives are mutinous! It is not like Europe and America.[20] Here, midwives fight to get what they want. But the biggest problem for us is that in the end, we are responsible for everything that goes on in the labor room. If there is a problem or a mistake, the obstetricians are held accountable for it." The doctor spoke of mutiny, of fighting, of responsibility and accountability. As in other medical contexts (Martin 1994), health professionals use the language of economy and war to talk about medicine and the body.

19. For a comparative description of policies and practices in Egypt, Palestine, Lebanon, and Syria, see Choices and Challenges for Changing Childbirth Research Network (2005). See also Maffi (2013).

20. This doctor thought that in European and American hospitals, midwives did not have much say in the assistance of childbirth.

Furthermore, midwives' narratives about work revolved around concepts of an everyday struggle contained in the notion of sumud. However, they integrated a critique of unacknowledged labor into the idea of sumud. Mirroring the political objectives of the Second Intifada, they directed their critique at both the occupation and the ruling class.

Sumud Practices of Phone Births and Dorm Life

At the most technologically advanced Palestinian hospital, Samia was not shy to say that half of her work of birthing assistance was done on the phone. She told stories resonating with experiences of health professionals throughout the Occupied Territories. Samia recalled a woman telephoning from a village under curfew: "Hello, I have contractions. I am afraid. I can't go to a hospital. We are under curfew," the woman said. "How many contractions per minute?" I asked. 'OK, take a shower and an Acamol [Tylenol] and try to sleep until morning, maybe you can find a way to come in the morning in daylight. But don't worry. Just don't be afraid. If worst comes to worst, I'll guide you and your family through delivery." In another conversation, the birthing woman said, "I have pain. I feel contractions. I can't wait anymore. The closure . . . I can't come. Help us!" So, I got the birthing woman's mother on the phone and tried to take them through delivery. I explained how to clamp the umbilical cord, to tie a string, to boil a pair of scissors, and then cut the cord."

The phone birth was unexpected in a hospital in Jerusalem, but became relatively common in areas under prolonged curfew. Through her accounts of phone births, Samia linked Jerusalem and the West Bank, which have been separated by the closure. In her story, assisting in phone births challenged the closure, connected her work to a resistant form of sumud, and bound her and her profession to people in the rest of Palestine. These stories illuminate a tension between the institutional, imposed, and lived separation of Jerusalem from the rest of Palestine and its unity and oneness with it, which is both imagined and willed, but also lived.

The administrative and physical partition of Jerusalem from the West Bank affected the midwives' own families, too. Except for those few residents of Jerusalem, they slept in the nurses' quarters at the hospitals to avoid the difficult roads. But they were unable to live with their families. Typically, they get one day off per week; however, in order to accumulate a few days' leave, they worked for four weeks without a break. They then went back to their hometown for four or five days. Samia was thirty-three, divorced, and had a daughter living in her village in the Ramallah district. Samia stayed in the nurses' dorms at Makassed on workdays. At the beginning of the intifada, she traveled to Jerusalem from her village every morning, but that proved impossible to continue. She had night shifts, sometimes two in a row. Then she moved to the nurses' dorms and would go back to see her daughter every two days, but the road was "crazy." Then she started going back every week. Even that became impossible during the long invasions of Ramallah. During the fieldwork for this study she could not even go back every week. In fact, she no longer obtained permits to come to Jerusalem and was in Jerusalem illegally. "Maybe the army thinks that because I am divorced and can't see my daughter very often, I am angry and may do something [violent]!" She felt guilty about not being able to see and take care of her daughter. Samia called her as soon as she got off work, sometimes wanting to quit her job. "But at least we bring money home. You know, I am always laughing. My daughter gives me motivation to stand strong on earth." The closure separated many midwives from their families. And after their shift, they would call their children and the families they left behind in other parts of the West Bank to connect.

Conclusion

Starting in the 1970s, with savvy diplomatic maneuvers and alliances, first Jordan, then the PLO started sending funds to charitable institutions and businesses inside the Occupied Territories. Social scientists have argued that this co-opted large swathes of the Palestinian public by transforming them into salaried personnel and consolidated the power of entrepreneurs and managers of the institutions. Charitable institutions and social networks are particularly important in Middle Eastern societies, as these forms of institutions have a deep historical presence since the late Ottoman period and are somewhat autonomous entities. Their presence complicates the theories of governmentality focusing on a relationship between the state and citizen subject. Based on fieldwork and interviews, I explored what it was like to work in sumud institutions. I illustrate the articulation of a particular vision of the nation through the institution and the functioning of a Palestinian hospital, Makassed, in Jerusalem. I also describe a type of nation that is unified, and technocratic, as envisaged by the doctor and contested by the midwife in the name of the people.

What the midwives contested was the assertion by the doctor that this particular national paradigm functioned smoothly and without major contradictions. Theirs were stories of unpaid, under-respected labor, carried out by working-class men and women. In these institutions, the various categories of health professionals live their daily travails as sumud. Doctors, like many in the Occupied Territories, see sumud as a practice, contrasting their definition of sumud to that of the PLO, for which it is a discourse and type of funding. They see their work of practicing medicine, struggling to get to their workplace, and managing these institutions as part of the work of sumud. They think of themselves as ethically and politically committed to the nationalist cause through their work, whereas nurses and midwives question the hospital model and criticize it for exploiting their labor. They redefine sumud to mean the work they perform with increased caseloads, decreased staffing, and the inability to visit their families often due to the closure. They always try to work against the closure in their own way. They use cell phone technology to assist births of women who are unable to reach Jerusalem, thereby symbolically reuniting a chopped-up land. And they call their children and families after their shifts in an effort to keep their families together. This for them is the work of sumud.

5

The Popular Health Movement and the Childbirth Network

Models in Participatory Health

In this chapter, I will turn to another type of health institution in Palestine that began with mass-based participatory health movements and gradually institutionalized to become NGOs. Through discussions with leading members of the movement, I will explore what participation looks like and what it means to people. In the late 1970s, a group of Palestinian doctors educated in the former Soviet Union started a health movement to resist Israeli occupation and break with the tradition of sumud institutions. They referred to themselves as *ṣumūd muqāwim* (resistant sumud), also known as the popular health movement. This movement adopted a model different from charitable associations, to which wealthy notables, businesspersons, and states donate to institutions that redistribute to the needy. Instead, they saw their work as addressing class inequalities by pushing people to demand health as a human right. The doctors themselves were part of a new class of leaders in Palestine. They were from rural backgrounds, although they lived in cities and were educated in the former Soviet Bloc. They started the movement by bringing mobile clinics to their homes and villages and then opening brick and mortar clinics in rural and underserved areas.

Many of the leaders of this movement I knew already. My mother had worked with them for a decade. And both my parents were their friends and colleagues. My parents had arrived in Palestine in 1983, after the Sabra and Shatila massacre, to work in solidarity with Palestinians. My father was a historian, professor, and a communist, and my mother a midwife and health researcher. Soon after their arrival, they started cooperating and working with the popular movements including in the health sector. The popular health movement stories blended with my own vivid memories of their work, as well as with photographs that my parents took. I remember both an atmosphere of hard work as well as one of festival, music, and politics, as shared with the internationalist cultures of leftist activism of the time. Today, most of the participants in this decentralized infrastructure had dispersed to the private and NGO sectors.

The healthcare infrastructure attached to *ṣumūd muqāwim* shows some differences from *sumud* institutions, especially in their distribution in rural and underserved areas and their beginnings as low-budget programs. They often began at the local level of the village, neighborhood, or camp, using a decentralized model that often emerged during a crisis, a long curfew, or siege, for example. With time, the clinics became part of the umbrella organization called the Union of Palestinian Medical Relief Committee (UPMRC), which in the late 1980s began to receive funding from international donors, rendering them into big organizations dependent on international funding. This and other changes led some leaders of the popular health movement to leave the UPMRC during the 1990s, citing the change of power dynamics as the organization grew as a result of increased outside funding. During the Second Intifada, however, they were compelled by the same energy to organize and assist with health services during sieges. Dr. Siham, for example, narrates the way the "childbirth network" organized to assist births during the closure. Nevertheless, some patients remain unhappy with the care they receive in villages and neighborhoods during the closures, narrate striking critiques of the health care they received, and continue to demand increased access.

Beginnings in the Mobile Clinic

The beginnings of the "popular health movement" emerged out of Makassed Hospital, where a group of newly trained physicians started volunteering once a week. They would pack their cars with a few medical supplies and drive from Makassed to underserved rural and refugee areas under curfew. Dr. Siham is one of the only women among the four founding members. She is from a village neighboring Ramallah and is the niece of a now deceased leader of the Communist Party. She talked about the philosophical and experiential influence that the popular health movement had on her current work in Ramallah. She started in the movement by offering a few hours per week of voluntary work in mobile clinics, treating patients free of charge. She and a group of physicians would drive around in their cars to villages with equipment and medication donated by local pharmacies and companies. Later, villagers offered them a room in the village to set up a permanent clinic. The physicians would rotate, offering one day per week of voluntary service and soon, more and more young doctors joined their group.

When Dr. Siham graduated from medical school in 1978, like any other doctor in Palestine she thought that the best thing for her would be to work and train in a hospital. During her work at Makassed, she noticed people came for treatments and cures, leaving only to return soon thereafter suffering from the exact same problem. One case she remembers well: A twenty-three-year-old woman named Ratiba came to her with a heart problem. When she gave birth, Dr. Siham barely saved her life and warned her that she should use contraception because all future births would be very dangerous. She lived close to Jerusalem, where Dr. Siham practiced, but would not continue with her care because she was under pressure from her community to have more children. She came back to her, pregnant, in her ninth month. Her heart was weak, and she died giving birth. She was an orphan herself. Her daughter survived the birth. Dr. Siham and the other medical personnel named her Ratiba like her mother. Ratiba still comes to Dr. Siham. She is about twenty now.

That case she will remember all her life, as it was a turning point in her personal and professional journey. She realized that without being in closer proximity to her patients, it was very difficult to provide for their care. At about this same time, a nascent idea was flourishing in the minds of young doctors (most working at Makassed hospital), the idea that they had to go to the people to provide care rather than the people coming to them. The first group event she remembers was in the late 1970s when Dheishe refugee camp, near Bethlehem, was under a prolonged curfew. She and a group of young doctors from Makassed took medication donated by a pharmacy and smuggled themselves and their bags into the camp. They went from house to house through backdoors and alleyways, seeing patients and visiting with their families. Then, after the curfew was lifted, people in the camp started asking for house visits. The same scenario took place in a village near Bethlehem and then in places farther away.

It became clearer to them that the health infrastructure was lacking a preventive system. The Israeli public health system in the Occupied Territories had a weak vision of prevention and the few Palestinian hospitals focused on curative care. In the years that followed, a series of committees began establishing community-based health clinics in underserved areas throughout the West Bank and Gaza to provide an alternative to Israeli and Palestinian hospitals. Mobile clinics sought to establish a decentralized, community-based health infrastructure to provide Palestinians with a viable alternative to Israeli government health provision and control. The new movement also sought to establish an alternative to biomedical and urban conceptions of health among doctors in the West Bank. Indeed, the mobile clinic faced opposition from the medical establishment at the time, as Dr. Riad, another main figure in the movement explained: "The idea of a mobile clinic was new, and they [the medical establishment] thought we were cheapening medicine. Seeing us carry our bags, they called us barbers."

It is at this time that some Makassed doctors and others formed the Union of Palestinian Medical Relief Committees (UPMRC, or Medical Relief). Their initial idea, and what they are still known for, is the mobile clinic. The doctors would take their cars and go to the Jordan valley, to the village of Deir Ghassaneh, to Bethlehem. Everyone would go together. The mobile clinics were conceived as an ad-hoc palliative to the centralized medical infrastructure. They promoted outreach to the remotest areas and introduced the notion of preventive and primary health care to the Occupied Territories. These clinics, after having been elaborated and utilized, tended to fade away with the proliferation of fixed primary healthcare centers. However, the outbreak of the December 1987 intifada created a new situation, and the mobile clinics were once again dispatched. During the Oslo period, they were again put aside in favor of a decentralized infrastructure of clinics. At the beginning of the 2000 intifada, Medical Relief deployed and reconceived the mobile clinics to cope with the closure. In the process, Dr. Rami noted, the very concept of the mobile clinic was transformed from its halting beginnings in 1979 to a chopped-up, decentralized, and professional infrastructure in the recent period. The basic idea, however, remained the same: "Reaching out to communities by providing health at their doorsteps."

I asked another doctor who had been involved in the popular health movement, Dr. Othman, to tell me about its beginnings. He told me that most of the doctors involved in the movement had just finished medical school in the Eastern bloc and appreciated certain public health programs in regions of the Soviet Union. Upon their return to the Occupied Territories, Dr. Othman explained, the ideology of the emergent popular health movement was still malleable and had not yet crystallized. The leading ideas that held the group together included "a national objective and a belief in justice." "We had energy," he said. "We wanted to do something for our country. We had all studied in the USSR or in other socialist countries during that period, and seen that health care was free of charge, whereas back home, people had to pay unaffordable prices for it. This was unjust. So, justice was our goal."

His story about the popular health movement's beginnings emphasized its spontaneity, popularity, and grassroots base and distanced the emergence of the group from the work of a political party. At the same time, Dr. Othman's account of the rapid and spontaneous mobilization of people around health also described popular health as mapping itself onto an existing social movement in the Occupied Territories. Their "entry points to the communities" in the rural areas were the activists in the women's movement, which had existed since the beginning of the twentieth century.[1] By the 1970s, the women's movement was active in social services, community organizing, and "was more powerful than us [the health movement]. We had little access to the communities we were targeting. They gave us the connections and the communities began to work with us." They did the relationship building and coordination until

---

1. For work on the Palestinian Women's Movement see Jad (1990, 2018); Hilterman (1991); Fleishman (2003); Hasso (2005); and Richter-Devroe (2018).

Medical Relief constructed its own organizational body. Dr. Othman, thus, inserts popular health into a genealogy of mass-based social movements in the Occupied Territories. He says that each local social movement was connected to the others. The women's organizations gave rise to and coexisted with the popular health movement. The popular health movement was accompanied by a similar agricultural and youth movement. These were essential for constructing the "neighborhood committees" during the First Intifada, which in turn solidified the Second Intifada when it erupted.[2] All of these movements and phases finally engendered the childbirth network.

At a time of disenchantment with party politics, Dr. Othman positions health within a genealogy of popular, mass-based movements rather than ideologies of parties and governments.[3] The final point regarding this story is that Dr. Othman's reference to "entry points into the communities" reveals a consciousness of the class division separating the doctors, who then became leaders of the movement, from the people they were trying to mobilize through health care. "We believed in health, social justice, and the participation of people in health care. The idea was that comprehensive primary health care pushes people to revolution. It would permit them to take power." With time, the vision became more specific to

2. The Palestinian intifada (uprising) against occupation broke out December 9, 1987, and spread throughout the Gaza Strip, Jerusalem, and the West Bank. In response, the Israeli army isolated towns, villages, and refugee camps from one another, in an attempt to clamp down on the always shifting, ever-active sequence of massive demonstrations, marches, and strikes. Frequent, brief, or prolonged sieges and curfews were regularly imposed throughout the country. The Palestinian population, in coordination with its leadership (The United National Leadership of the Intifada, or UNLU) quickly established localized, grassroots neighborhood (or "popular") committees tasked with ensuring basic services in various essential areas, including health, education, supplies, security, agriculture, and information. Their importance during the early years of the 1987–93 uprising was considerable, and they were effective for varying periods depending on place. They had to go underground when Israel declared them illegal and threatened ten-year imprisonment for their members. For more on popular committees, see Heacock and Nassar (1990).

3. For more on the pre-intifada period, see Taraki (1990).

the context of Palestine. What made the movement instantly popular, Dr. Othman said, was that people saw it as a means of resistance to occupation. "Health was controlled by the Israeli authorities. They decided whom to hire, whom not to hire, whom to treat, whom not to treat, what to do, what not to do. Therefore, developing health services without the permission of the authorities was a challenge to occupation." In Dr. Othman's stories, the illegal status of the popular health movement was essential to the creation of its popular base (see also Barghouti and Giacaman 1990). Indeed, the illegality of the popular health movement stood in contrast to the politics of health in the sumud-based charitable hospitals. The leaders of the movement position it in stark and proactive opposition to the Israeli politics of health in the Occupied Territories but also to the centralizing and legalistic politics of health promoted by the PLO.

The health system is a microcosm of this socially based vision. They modeled decentralized health care and questioned the primacy of the Ministry of Health. The village health worker, introduced by the UPMRC in the late 1980s, became a significant figure of the popular health movement. The system was looser, broader, and in theory, less subject to vertical control. Dr. Othman went on to recount the bureaucratization of the movement about a decade after its emergence and the role the political parties played in this process. The umbrella organization, the UPMRC, became an entity over which political parties sought control and, subsequently, internal disagreements started to emerge. Members from Fatah and the Popular Front seceded and created similar organizations, but close to their own parties, and the UPMRC was left to the Communist Party.[4] In his story, the first decade of the movement was exciting and popular, whereas the second phase was tainted by the politics of bureaucracies, internal power struggles, and political parties.

4. Fatah is the hegemonic Palestinian nationalist party, headed by Yasser Arafat until his death in November 2005, and then by Mahmud Abbas (Abu Mazen), elected to succeed him as president of the PA. The PFLP is a Marxist, pan-Arab party considered more intransigent than Fatah. The Palestinian Communist Party (now renamed Palestinian People's Party), unlike Fatah and the PFLP, always favored a two-state solution for Palestine.

Dr. Siham, for her part, had long been a leading person in the popular health movement and politically involved. Her interview had the aura of a political speech. After leaving the UPMRC, she joined a practice in downtown Ramallah. However, when the closure of the second intifada started, she said, the childbirth network reenergized her. It brought back the memories and passion she had found in her initial work with the UPMRC. Like Dr. Siham, Dr. Othman spoke from the perspective of someone who had been very active in the former health movement, but now worked in the nongovernmental organization sector. They took pride in their past involvement in the health movement.

Another leading figure in the popular health movement who then became the UPMRC director, Dr. Riad emphasized what he thought were the exceptional qualifications of Palestinian doctors in creating original movements in the 1970s. Professionally, they had the necessary skills. Politically, they had acquired a broad socialist vision. Socioeconomically, they came from previously deprived rural and refugee classes and were in the process of replacing the existing medical elite composed of urban notables. The founding members all noted that practicing medicine in underserved areas put them back in touch with Palestinian society, from which their long years of academic training and social ascension had somewhat distanced them. Importantly, when Dr. Riad refers to their rural classes, he is drawing on opposition to the long-established urban elites, but he is also speaking of their roots. For example, he is from a land-owning (*iqta'*) family of Deir Ghassaneh; he never lived there (he grew up in neighboring El-Bireh and now lives in Ramallah), but he maintained family, political, and professional ties to his village. It is in this sense that he identifies the group of physicians as having more organic ties to the communities they served. Thus, their connection to rural areas strengthens their ties to the land, place, and people.

By the mid-1980s, the UPMRC started opening clinics in villages and developed the concept of "permanent care," in addition to having mobile clinics. "In 1985, we started thinking about women's health. We started having clinics specifically for the prevention of cancer and promotion of women's health," Dr. Siham said. The first village where they opened this kind of clinic was Deir Ghassaneh. "In 1987, we started our training

for 'village health workers' and women doctors who had recently graduated. We did not have a clear idea of the training, but we wanted it to be
centered on women's health. Many of the ideas came from the women
who had enrolled in the program. Then they started reading and hearing
about experiences with this kind of training elsewhere." Dr. Siham, like
many other doctors, did not know what daily life was like in the villages.
Although she is originally from a village and has maintained ties, her work
with the UPMRC exposed her to daily village life, to poorer villages, and
to poorer classes within villages. She learned a lot from the women in self-
training. Then, when she went to the clinics in the villages, she looked for
what the young women described. They told her that the physical illnesses
of women often had a basis in psychological health, things they could
not talk about with their doctors because they would not understand or
because customs say that the good woman is the woman who is silent and
does not speak of pain. With experience, Dr. Siham and her colleagues
at the women's health clinics saw a marked increase in women who just
wanted to talk. It is at this point that they decided that women needed
regular contact with health professionals and psychological care. Therefore, she trained ten women doctors and health workers in psychological
care. The women's health program grew to about twenty-three clinics and
saw thousands of patients. She thinks it was the most successful program
at Medical Relief.

Along with the program of training village health workers, the wom-
en's health program had grown to become so important within Medical
Relief that all the founding members wanted to be a part of it. However,
over time Dr. Siham and Dr. Othman explained to me, Medical Relief
changed. In the beginning years when their work was on a smaller scale,
they described a space of teamwork and shared decision-making. They
would disagree about what the priorities should be, but then the steering
committee would vote, and the organization would move forward with
the decision. At this time in the early eighties, entire infrastructures were
thus built (schools, clinics, agricultural cooperatives). During the entire
formative period, which lasted over a decade, the UPMRC had no donors;
they volunteered and used their own funds to collect the material they
required. They also had fundraising parties that collected sums which, at

the time, were considered considerable, as much as $15,000, Dr. Othman told me. However, with the growth of the organization, and as it received more funding, it changed. Funders wanted one person to be responsible for the funds and the director became the sole decision-maker. "He started to decide to what projects the funding would go. He was the one who knew about the funding. It became a very centralized organization. We had become this big organization, with big clinics and many employees, and any micro-decision had to be taken by one person. In the 1990s, it started to develop into a power struggle among the founders. By the mid-to-late '90s, many of us left." She described an organization that was increasingly difficult to work within because it had lost its culture of communal work and shared decision-making.[5]

Furthermore, party politics played out in the organization. As the membership increasingly tilted toward Communists, others and notably Popular Front for the Liberation of Palestine (PFLP) and Fatah left Medical Relief and created their own versions (the PFLP created the *lijān al-'amal al-ṣaḥī*, "Health Work Committees" and Fatah the *lijān al-khadamāt al-ṣaḥīyya*, or "Health Services Committees"). Fatah, in particular, was anxious through their Health Services Committees to assert political hegemony at the grassroots level and invested considerable money to that end. In the short run, Fatah created over 120 clinics, but given lack of resources, they were soon reduced to twenty, and then closed down altogether as Fatah placed its resources in other areas, such as unions and youth groups. There was a new political surge in the health field, coinciding with the 1987 intifada when the governmental infrastructure broke down, each party individually and all of them together stepping in to fill the breech. The UPMRC was in every respect the model and source of what then became a generalized interest in public health.

By the 1990s, many of the founding members of the popular health movement left the UPMRC. Dr. Siham left in 1996 and opened a private practice in Ramallah. Dr. Othman left to work in an international

---

5. For other accounts of NGOization in Palestine, see Hammami (1995), and Hanafi and Tabar (2005).

nongovernmental organization. It was not until the Second Intifada that they felt the excitement and purpose in their work again through their efforts to put together a "childbirth network" to assist births during the siege.

Childbirth Care: The Problem of Access

As checkpoints and closures proliferated after the beginning of the Second Intifada in 2000, restricting movement inside the West Bank as well as referrals to Jerusalem, health workers living in villages became essential to assisting births. Until the closures, women had access through a network of primary health care clinics and hospitals in towns. Although service quality is inadequate in the public sector, 99 percent of births are attended by skilled personnel, with 15 percent resulting in caesarean section (Abdel-Rahim et al. 2009) and a maternal mortality ratio of 46/100,000 live births (Hogan et al. 2010). In contrast to some post-conflict areas such as East Timor, where the number of physicians remaining in the country was reduced from 135 to 20, and Iraq and Syria (Alonso and Brugha 2006), the physician ratio in Palestine is higher (2.1 per 1,000) but poorly distributed, with the public sector lacking in numbers and competence.

As of 1994 and continuing previous Israeli policy, the Palestinian health authorities urged pregnant women to stop giving birth at home with community midwives and instead to deliver in government hospitals. To this end, the Palestinian Authority (PA) stopped issuing any new licenses to *dayāt*, the trained birth attendants who were delivering babies in villages. Those with licenses could continue practicing, but no new *dayāt* would be licensed. Thus, over time, the dayat were aging and there were fewer and fewer. To accommodate the needs of poor families (57 percent of the population in 2007: Mataria et al. 2009), the PA introduced a free insurance scheme for births in government hospitals, where subsequently over one-half of births took place.[6] By 1999, 99 percent of births took place in a hospital located in towns or cities (Abdel-Rahim et al. 2009).

6. Ten percent of the budget of the Palestinian Authority (based primarily on foreign donations) goes to the Ministry of Health, with a per person expenditure of $135 (Mataria et al. 2009).

The journey from villages to the hospital in a town became a necessary part of labor and delivery, but in 2000, the closure tightened, and it became difficult to travel from villages to towns. In a time when a biomedical and modernizing discourse had persuaded people that hospitals were the only safe place for birth, women were faced with the dilemma of unpredictable access to maternity hospitals.[7] According to the Palestinian Ministry of Health, between 2000 and 2005, sixty-nine cases were reported of Palestinian women giving birth at checkpoints, with four maternal and thirty-four neonatal deaths (Office of the High Commissioner for Human Rights 2005). I interpret these numbers to be so high because of stress and fear that accompanied women's deliveries. But also, I think that if women were attempting to get to the hospital during a siege, curfew, or severe closure, they were probably in emergency situations with high-risk deliveries. Had the labor been normal, the women probably would have opted to give birth in clinics in their villages or possibly at home.

In response to poor access to hospitals, health professionals created the network, or *shabaka*, to assist births during the closure. They shared experiences and expertise and put together a birthing hotline to assist women over the telephone who could not make it to a maternity facility (Wick 2008). In our interview, Dr. Siham spoke of the popular health movement with nostalgia and pride, but it is the contemporary stories of the birth clinics and networks that she was most excited about. This network considers itself an offshoot of the popular health movement and began organizing during the second intifada to assist births during the closure.

The Network

The streets were empty. The stores were closed. The people were indoors. The only sound the city made was the roaring of passing tanks. Ramallah

---

7. Countries such as Egypt, Jordan, and Lebanon have also undergone a process of hospitalization of birth, accompanied by an increasing privatization of medicine, a diminished role for midwives in relation to male physicians, a rising caesarean section rate, and lack of routine evidence-based childbirth practices (Choices and Challenges in Changing Childbirth Research Network 2005).

was silent. Since March 29, 2002, the Israeli army had imposed a curfew on Ramallah. For the first two months, it was very strict. People never broke it. Every few days, the army lifted the curfew for a few hours so that people could stock up on food. Later, the curfew was less strict and was lifted more often. People sat on their verandas. Children played in the streets. But at the sound of the tanks, everyone went running inside. Then, on the morning of July 4, 2002, Ramallah was bustling. The whole city was in the streets. Vegetable vendors, sandal and shoe sellers, shoppers and strollers mingled in the middle of town. Political leaders and prisoners— Marwan Barghouti, Ahmad Saadat, as well as intifada martyrs, Wafa' Idris, Muhammad al-Durra—looked down from posters on the walls.[8] There was not a soldier in sight. Cell phones were ringing everywhere. Horns were honking. Radios were blasting. Ramallah was loud; the curfew had been lifted.

In an office building at the center of town, Dr. Siham shared a private clinic with a few other health professionals. The building was empty, the door barely open. She was alone in her clinic, talking on the phone: "You'll be fine. The curfew is lifted until 2:00 p.m. You can stop by the clinic if you want, before then. But I don't think it's necessary. Call me at home if you feel pain." Dr. Siham turned to me and said: "I would never have imagined that I would practice medicine by phone . . . I never thought I would wake up at 2:00 a.m. to phone calls from women in labor and instruct the husband how to assist his wife in childbirth. I have never heard of a time in history when even health providers were restricted in their movements. But the thing is, life goes on. Women still become sick. Women still become pregnant. They can impose a curfew, restrict mobility, but it does not stop labor from starting. This is dangerous. This is frightening."

8. Marwan Barghouti: A popular, elected member of the Palestinian Legislative Council sentenced to life imprisonment by Israel, head of the militant Tanzim within Fatah, which contested the bureaucratic and corrupt leadership as well as the occupation. Ahmad Saadat: Leader of the Popular Front for the Liberation of Palestine (PFLP). Wafa' Idris: The first Palestinian woman suicide bomber. Muhammad al-Durra: A child killed by Israeli gunfire in his father's arms at the beginning of the Second Intifada, on September 30, 2000.

The phone rang again. It was another patient. In between periods of medical advice given on the phone to her patients, Dr. Siham told me stories about assisting birth by phone during curfew nights. She explained that this instrument had become a crucial medium of medical assistance. Since many women thought it better to give birth at home than to brave the curfew, they would telephone health providers to get counseling during childbirth. Dr. Siham's stories centered on a movement of health professionals who had mobilized to provide services to women who went into labor during curfews:

> Sort of naturally, by the first days of the curfew, many health providers in the Ramallah area would converse, share stories, and give each other advice. Quickly and spontaneously, we had a system working. Health providers would tell people in need to call such and such a person to follow up on something. Those with no experience with childbirth in a village under siege would call me so I could give them training by phone . . . Since the beginning of the long invasion we have created a hotline to provide this network of medical services and advice, so we can take many midwives, nurses, and lay people through childbirth on the phone.

They trained at least one person to assist births in each neighborhood or village. The trainee could be a doctor, midwife, nurse, health worker, or lay person. There was excitement in her voice when she talked about the network. Through the childbirth network, she felt that she regained her trust and enthusiasm for mass participation after six years of working in the private sector and lamenting that the days of activism in healthcare might be gone.

The phone rang again, and a few patients had come into her clinic. She talked to the phone patient, and then saw her clinic patients. In the midst of this chaos, while expecting the curfew to be reimposed any minute, she told me stories of an effective and active "childbirth network." For Dr. Siham, the network would bring childbirth close to women's homes or neighborhoods:

With this hotline and network, we are also trying to convince women to have natural childbirth at home or close to the woman's home.[9] That way, we can avoid the fear, humiliation and danger of the road . . . So, I try to convince women to forget about the hospital. That it is safer for them to give birth close to where they live . . . If we create a system where women can give birth close to their homes, that is what I mean by natural childbirth, then we would have succeeded in something extraordinary for our political aspirations."

She wanted women to relocate birthing back to their villages, where they were prior to the mass medicalization of childbirth in the early 1990s. Her goal was to build a lasting, decentralized infrastructure and make each neighborhood self-sufficient. She thought of this network as a continuation of the popular health movement of the 1980s, carrying its ideas of decentralization, popular health, primary healthcare, and equality. During our conversation, the phone rang every few minutes. Two patients wandered into her clinic for a visit. All of us felt that the time was almost up. At this point, we heard the army's microphone calling out: "Curfew, curfew. Go home."

I left this first interview with a sense of enchantment about the grassroots efforts in the medical field, and with a sense of fascination with the image she conveyed of doctors as fighters and leaders. I visited many midwives and some doctors who had home practices in villages to assist births during the closure. Most had heard of the network. Often organizers in the network had contacted them to map out the sites where people could give birth if in need and to integrate them into a directory of people who assisted

---

9. It became clear as her story proceeded that the meanings of "natural childbirth" for her were different from the meanings attached to it in the United States. For Dr. Siham, natural childbirth is not so much about giving birth without technologies and drugs as about locating the birth in women's neighborhoods rather than in large, urban hospitals. Dr. Siham's definition of natural childbirth was different from what *wilāda ṭabiʻiyya* meant in common language. When people usually talked about births being *ṭabiʻiyya*, natural, they meant to say that it was what in medicine is called a "normal" birth, meaning the regular length of pregnancy and a spontaneous, vaginal birth.

births. But these home-practice health workers did not necessarily describe themselves as being part of the network. Several responded adamantly that they were not part of any network or movement, but were simply doing their duty of being decent health workers. They distanced themselves from the term "network." "What network?" a young doctor working in the out-skirts of Ramallah asked me, "I'm just doing my job." I interpret such dis-tancing from the network as part of a more generalized disenchantment with organized politics and movements, and to comment that all parts of the infrastructure are problematic, no part is morally superior.

The conversations about social movements and networks made me think of the social science work on networks. Since the 1990s, scholars have talked about "networks" (Castells and Portes 1989) to describe how people participate politically and cooperate outside the formal political system. Arjun Appadurai (2006) makes a distinction between "vertebrate" (hierarchical, arborescent) and "cellular" (networked, rhizomatic) social forms. States are the main bearers of a vertebrate form. They always rely on fixed, regulative norms and signals, which function like a trunk. The fear of cellular opposition groups provides excuses for state intrusion into civil society. The state pursues a kind of war in everyday life against cellu-lar power structures. Appadurai thus creates a sense of a global social war between state forces and networked social forces. It is in Appadurai's sense of a cellular social force that I use the term "network."

However, the case of Palestine shows that no matter how informal or spontaneous a network is, some find it already too institutionalized and hierarchical. Indeed, the fact that many doctors and midwives refused to identify with the term network, yet did the collaborative work of as-sisting births in makeshift clinics, shows the ways in which they iden-tified the institutional and ideological nature of that network. Because most institution-building in Palestine developed through social move-ments and networks that worked against the state (controlled by the Is-raeli military), the notion of formal versus informal when applied to such networks is tinged with ambiguity. Some health workers were seeing the same recursive structures in all the different movements in health care: leaders lead, managers manage, workers work. From the highest levels to the smallest of "informal" networks, they saw them as institutionalized, hierarchical, and ideological. People chose not to align themselves with a network to avoid working in the service of political parties, movements, or institutions. They worked in health assistance but did not want to be allied with a social movement or network. As noted before, perhaps their work would be better understood as a "cellular" (Appadurai 2006) form of organizing. Cellular organizations, unlike "vertebrate" organizations, such as nation-states, are flexible and less hierarchical. They bring together a small number of participants who work together based on a shared number of principles, rather than on command by decision-making structures of armies (Appadurai 2006). The doctors not wanting to be part of a network suggests a kind of fatigue and disillusionment with ideology and political movements all together. They just want to do the work well and have it be what it is without it having a political agenda. This nonpolitical stance is also political. In a highly political landscape, it's impossible to escape. Every subject position becomes political in one way or another.

Medical institutions and professions are part of a wider political mood in Palestinian society. Anthropologists and other social scientists have written about the general political attitude of being fed up with the futility of politics and pervasive suffering (Allen 2013), of the mistrust of political parties among refugees in the diaspora (Allan 2014), and the discontent about unequal access to small compensations distributed by municipalities and political parties (Malki 2005). Whereas in the 1980s, when the popular health movement was active, everyone was either close to or a member of a political party, by the Second Intifada in 2000, some people did not want to be involved in party politics and distanced themselves from them.

Feisty Critiques of Care

New mothers often spoke about birth assistance during the closure and the way health workers organized to assist births. In the beginning of this book, I wrote about new mothers' feelings of isolation and loss after birth. In this section, I want to highlight some new mothers' feisty critiques of the medical care they received and the effects it had on the doctors, clinics, and hospitals offering the care.

Some had painful stories of the care they received and criticized health workers. Maha, for example, whose story I narrated at the beginning of the book, had arranged to give birth at Red Crescent Hospital in Ramallah. In early April 2002, however, the severe curfew made it highly unlikely that she could make it there and back. She wondered, "If I got to the hospital, how long would it take me before I could come back? What about my husband and children alone at home? I was afraid the soldiers might come to arrest my husband . . . So, I was afraid the kids might be alone. I thought about it a hundred times." Maha had heard from a neighbor that a doctor who lived in her neighborhood was assisting births in her home. Eventually, she decided to give birth with this doctor.

"At 6:30 p.m., on the 14th of April, I went to [the doctor's] house with my neighbor. My cervix was dilated 3.5 cm. The doctor said, 'In about two hours, you will give birth.' So, she did things to facilitate my birth. At 9:30, I gave birth to my daughter. Quickly, she cleaned me up. I had a tear, but she did not stitch me up . . . She made me understand that we were bothering her. She kicked us out!" Maha was upset as she explained how she gave birth in a room in a doctor's home turned birthing clinic and very soon after the birth, the doctor made her feel unwelcome. So, she and her neighbor picked up the newborn and walked home. On the way, they heard a tank approaching, so they knocked at the door of a house to ask for cover. "The people did not just open the door for us," she explained, "they had us sit down and made us some tea, and we started talking. 'How did the doctor let you leave when you had barely given birth?' the hosts asked us. Even though I had a tear. See how lowly of the doctor! The doctor has no principles. Conversing with her hosts, Maha shared her story of how the doctor had requested from her to leave right after delivery and they shared their outrage. "After drinking tea and chatting with us," she continued, "the hosts telephoned the houses along the main road. Young men looked out from their roofs. If a tank came, they would whistle. This way we got home." She narrated how strangers who lived in her neighborhood welcomed her and then they and others assisted her in getting back home. In contrast to the doctor, people who lived in her neighborhood were in solidarity with her.

One element of Maha's story is part of a collective narrative about life under curfew. She, her neighbor, and her newborn baby dodged tanks in the middle of the night. She hid in the house of a hospitable family she did not even know, and the young men in the neighborhood worked out a system of watching and whistling so they could run safely to their home. It is the story of neighborhood cooperation, one reminiscent of popular movement stories from the First Intifada. In her story, the doctor (whom, incidentally, Dr. Siham would likely consider part of the childbirth network) was not part of the popular movement. Maha's tone was one of anger. She kept on repeating that the doctor was greedy, inhospitable, and in the end, did not have the morals a doctor should have nor the politics someone under curfew should have. She had paid for the service and expected assistance during and for a few hours after birth in return. She was staunchly critical of the medical care she received and the doctor who assisted her. The story others told was similar in structure: she broke the curfew during the night and was helped by the neighborhood to get back and forth from the doctor's house, but the doctor was inhumane and did not tend to Maha's tear. Such stories and retellings propagated critiques of medical assistance, and doctors in particular.

I regularly heard stories blaming doctors in clinics and hospitals for poor medical care. These stories had tangible effects on doctors, clinics, and hospitals. One example is Dr. T's clinic in a village near Ramallah. Founded in 1970 by women's popular committees, this vaccination clinic ran projects on the modest profit derived from women's volunteer work selling agricultural produce and embroidery. It also received a modicum of financial support from a local church and, beginning in the late 1980s, small donations from development organizations, although there are no financial records of this. When the PA arrived in 1994, the clinic's local funding dried up, even as most international aid went to the new government. Dr. T also had a private clinic in Ramallah that she ran before the beginning of the extensive closures. According to her and others I interviewed in her village in 2002, she was asked by anxious pregnant women, who foresaw difficulties in accessing hospitals in Ramallah, to assist births in the villages. There had been sieges and long closures on Nablus and

Hebron and most cities of the West Bank and so it was reasonable to think that it might happen in Ramallah. When the first woman came to ask her if she would assist her birth in the village in the event of a closure, Dr. T did not take her seriously. She was an obstetrician, trained to do operations and assist births with complications. She had only assisted births in hospitals complete with technologies, nursing staff, operating rooms, and specialized physicians. When a second and then a third woman asked if she would assist their births if their labor started at a time of closure, Dr. T decided to prepare herself. She packed scissors, sterilizers, cotton, gauze, and gloves—the necessary equipment for a delivery—and put them in her village clinic, which had been closed for a few years.

Neither Dr. T nor anyone else foresaw the scale of the closure. Her own village, dependent on the infrastructure of schools, markets, and hospitals in Ramallah, was now isolated from it for months on end. She delivered the baby of the first woman in the village a few days after the beginning of the incursion with the help of a volunteer nurse. After the first birth, the mother went home announcing that she had had a better experience at the clinic than in any hospital. Word spread, and Dr. T assisted in more and more births. A week after she had assisted the first birth in her village, the village council called upon key people in the neighboring villages and declared Dr. T's clinic as the emergency center for women in labor who managed to reach it.[10] They printed pamphlets about the clinic and distributed them in nearby villages. Dr. T was the only obstetrician in the area and received practically all the pregnant patients. She assisted eighty births between March 29 and May 5, 2002.

After three weeks of the closure and no prospect that the road to Ramallah would reopen, she worried about potential complications and decided to try to get donations for more expensive equipment. The four doctors with private clinics in the neighboring villages brought her all their basic materials, such as cotton and gloves. Two local pharmacies brought her sterilizers and other supplies. She also received donations

10. On the resurgence of village councils during the Second Intifada, see Malki (2005).

from Palestinian organizations in Israel, which permitted her to buy oxygen cylinders, IV drips, and the drug oxytocin, used to induce labor and prevent or treat hemorrhage after birth. Ethnographies of medical services in poor settings show that this method of resorting to donations is central to their survival (Biehl 2005), and especially crucial to health economies in war areas. Health workers and patients also often arrived at the clinic with some of the supplies needed for a birth. Dr. T developed what she called a system of legal protection by asking the husbands to stay with their wives during labor and delivery. In this way, the husband was able to see what was going on and the efforts that she put into her work. In case of a problem, he would be a witness.

In time, Dr. T's village practice became exhausting. It was too much work and responsibility for one doctor. Some nights she did not sleep, while other nights, she slept on the couch in the clinic. She experienced excessive pressure daily. I visited the clinic and village as often as I could. On one of my visits, Dr. T seemed worried. During one of the births, assisted by Dr. T., a villager's newborn died. "The whole village is talking about a problem we had," she told me. "But what could we do? We were ill-equipped and unprepared to assist births in our clinic." According to her and to some people in the village I saw later, the villagers blamed the doctor for the newborn's death. Eventually, a month after my interview with Dr. T, villagers told me that she had left the village. Tamara, one of the women who gave birth to a healthy baby in the village during this period of closure, voiced further criticism of this doctor. Tamara had given birth in her home, unexpectedly early. Her husband called Dr. T right away and "it took a whole hour for the doctor to come and cut the umbilical cord. And she lives close by," Tamara told me with a tone of reproach. She was bitter about the childbirth assistance her village was offered and blamed the doctor personally. In such an atmosphere, with stories about her poor practice circulating in her village, Dr. T closed the village clinic for eighteen months.

Some new mothers' critiques of the medical care they received during birth take me full circle back to the beginning of the book. New mothers had a sense of loss and loneliness after giving birth and some actively criticized the care they received during birth. The critiques took the form of stories told and retold to me and other listeners. The doctors and hospital administrators felt that the stories quickly turned to rumors blaming their practice or institution and often had to close a clinic temporarily or fire a doctor. Through scandal and rumor, new mothers and their communities disrupted the health infrastructure. Physicians feared the scandals and rumors and tried to institute informal ways of dealing with the risk of being accused of malpractice. For example, Dr. T. explained that she always demanded that there be a male witness, such as the woman's husband, so that they could attest to her efforts and hard work.

Conclusion

Through interviews with founding members, this chapter narrates the history of the popular health movement starting in the late 1970s. The movement worked against the model of the central urban hospital developed by sumud institutions by decentralizing health care to villages, camps, and other underserved areas. The founding members narrated the beginnings of the movement that brought people from diverse backgrounds together with a sense of solidarity. Their first attempts to reach underserved and isolated communities was with the mobile clinic. Gradually, with time, they opened physical clinics in villages. In the meantime, the movement slowly transformed itself into an institution, characterized by a large workforce, a hierarchical governing body, and dependence on foreign funding. In the 1990s, many of the founding members left, disappointed in the Medical Relief Committees, and opened private practices or worked in international non-governmental organizations.

With the beginning of the Second Intifada in 2000, health workers organized to assist births during the closure. These efforts reignited the former leaders of the popular health movement's passion and excitement in community health care. They saw in these efforts the spontaneity and mass participation that the Medical Relief Committees had lost. In collaboration with others, they founded a network of health professionals who assisted births during the closure and kept connected over the phone. That said, many health workers who assisted births during the closure did not consider themselves part of the network, but rather that they were just doing their jobs. No matter how informal and spontaneous a network is, some find it already too institutionalized and hierarchical, a symptom of fatigue and disillusionment with organized political movements.

In the end of the chapter, I circle back to interviews and participant observation with mothers who gave birth and highlight their stark criticism of the care they received. They felt mistreated by health professionals, and doctors in particular. They and other community members circulated birth stories that transformed into rumor and then local scandals. These rumors and scandals disrupted the medical infrastructure, at least temporarily, and reiterated communities' demand for better access to medical care.

Conclusion

As I began meeting women who had given birth, I was intrigued by their intense sense of loss. They were caring for a new baby, rethinking their familiar relationships, remembering their childhoods, and trying to maintain normalcy while finding meaning in their present condition. My ethnography has followed those relationships to see each of them as separate but also connected. I have gone from site to site to share the impression of my fieldwork: new mothers in their homes, midwives in hospitals and dorms, a bustling waiting room with people trying to enter the hospital, a group of doctors discussing the heyday of the popular health movement, hospital labor rooms with many laboring women, and small village clinics with a single bed, an IV, and a doctor. In retrospect, my fieldwork took me from one set of questions to another. In each step, I attempt to understand how people tell their stories, with what shared patterns, and in what ways they are divided, ambiguous, and disjunctive. These passages reveal intimate experiences about life, people, anthropology, and my place in all of it.

When I started fieldwork exploring childbirth in 2002, I began by studying the childbirth network and the different forms of organization of medicine and childbirth care in times of crisis and siege. But during that fieldwork, I met Maha and other new mothers and got acquainted with the world they lived in, and my own intellectual and emotional world slowly began to change. It was not the close friendships with new mothers that caused this to happen. Rather it was the broader view of their worlds I had access to through them—a world concealed behind terms we use in everyday discourse, terms like "war," "medicine," "humanitarian assistance," "closure," and "occupation." I realized that public health institutions did not merely provide healthcare and that different segments of society told different types of stories about similar events. I began to see that not just personalities and organizations, but local small-scale histories mattered too. For example, public health and medicine use universal models and terminology, but there is a whole world organized around birth in a village clinic, a community hospital labor ward, or a home. And in these sites, concepts are shaped to fit the local context and groups of people tell different types of stories about it. New mothers told birth stories about loss and love; midwives insisted I record their oral histories, while their brothers and husbands did not; and doctors and health care workers told stories about sumud and the creation of healthcare infrastructure. Some questioned the sumud model and others did not want to be associated with any political movement at all.

Back then, I spent most of my time in Ramallah, a town I would return to many times over the course of writing this book, because as a regional center in the West Bank, it had many sites for giving birth. People from its rural hinterlands came seeking healthcare and administrative affairs in state institutions, schooling, commerce, and leisure. New mothers often spoke of their contact with the regional center as one of neglect or failure; they came seeking care, but the commute was long because of checkpoints and the care they received was unkind. Therefore, women chose to give birth in their new villages, separated from healthcare infrastructure and from their families of origin who lived in other villages.

The closure, with its checkpoints, barricades, hierarchy of IDs, restrictions on mobility, and its separation of towns and villages, structured everyone's daily experience, but in different ways. New mothers felt like they were losing relationships with their families of origin because they could not visit often due to these restrictions. Midwives needed to sleep in hospital dorms in order to work and were sometimes unable to see their children for weeks on end. Doctors spent a few hours per day on the road and some worked in building up the public health system. Questions of access and coping with the closure were important for how these doctors thought of the public health system. Indeed, while everyone seemed to have the collective feeling that their worlds were being reduced, peoples' stories about such experiences differed.

Thus, I set out to write about how a diverse set of people living under similar conditions tell stories of birth and new beginnings as they grapple with the effects of seeing their worlds reduced. The primary challenge of writing this book was analyzing the patterns in the stories I collected, while bringing to light the tensions that permanently erode them. For example, I noticed that midwives told oral histories with a similar narrative arc, but then when I listened carefully, at certain points the narratives are interrupted and dislocated, and I tried to piece together the meaning of that disjuncture. The mothers, midwives, doctors, sumud hospitals, the popular health movement, and the village clinics I examine in these pages are far from being well-bounded clusters of stories and places with straightforward meanings. The stories and places are unstable, disconnected, and made and unmade through different processes at different moments in time. For example, looking at the infrastructure of health, the most striking aspect I had to deal with as an ethnographer was how rapidly it changed. I collected a set of stories about a neonatal death in a village clinic, which had repercussions on the village clinic. For months, the doctor stopped coming to the village for fear of retaliation. Then, a year later, the doctor returned with funding from international organizations to open a birthing clinic and the stories around the clinic had changed, too. What is particular in stories about health infrastructures in crisis is the pace at which they change.

Throughout my fieldwork, I learned from new mothers what it means to have recently given birth with a sense of self that was changed. I was surprised to hear stories about loss and loneliness because the anthropology of birth, on the one hand, focuses on medicalization. And the social science literature, on the other hand, focuses on loneliness and its connections to industrialization, capitalism, and urbanization. Yet there is a shared experience, common to many around the world, with displacement, exile, and closed borders affecting huge parts of the world population. This shared experience can be captured neither by medicalization nor by industrialization. The analyses of the narratives of loss and loneliness shed light on these experiences. For example, Rama tells a story about loneliness and love. She longs for the support her parents used to provide for her before her marriage. She spends most of her days alone, caring for her three daughters. The only person she sees is her sister-in-law. Hibah too tells a story centered on love, loss, and loneliness. She experiences the period after birth as an intense meaning-making period. Her parents who live in a neighboring village cannot visit her often because of the closure and she feels the loss of relationships and that her world is becoming smaller and more isolated.

Midwives told different kinds of stories and insisted I collect their oral histories. Tahrir and Suhaila narrated their unique stories, which were characteristic of the genre of oral histories: clear, consistent, and typical in terms of plot and tone. They referred to places, dates, and political events, but in certain moments of the recording, there were ruptures in the clear narrative. For Tahrir, dates, time, and stories became jumbled when she spoke of her divorce. She viewed herself as a strong and struggling person and as surely able to transmit that strength to her children. However, her years of separation from her children made her question her sense of self and, at the time of the recording, it remained uncertain how often she would get to see her children and, thus, how much she could influence them. While Suhaila did not face a deep sense of crisis like Tahrir's separation from her children, her narrative too had moments of disjuncture and shifts into what sounded like jumbled speech or epic poetry. "Ottomans killed rebellious hearts," she said at one point in her chronological and clear narrative. I interpreted Suhaila's interjection at the end of a realist anecdote to be a sentence she borrowed from the *qiṣa* genre, a storytelling genre now practiced mainly in rural areas, focused on the deeds and adventures of heroic figures of the past. It was a way for her to fill a moment of silence and mask the confusion and difficulty she experienced narrating a realist oral history structured by important dates and political events.

Midwives were using a well-known genre in Palestine that emerged after 1967 when the PLO modeled its struggle on anti-colonial movements, many of which had instituted large state-run oral history projects. However, unlike the oral history projects of newly independent postcolonial countries, Palestinian oral history was not a state project. It was a decentralized effort. Starting in the 1970s, intellectuals, village councils, teachers, and their students practiced oral history. The medium spread quickly. Oral history was distributed as pamphlets in schools and workshops. The oral historians were conservationist and aimed to maintain local traditions and histories. They thought of themselves as preserving traditional ways of life that continued to disappear since the 1948 dislocation and the persistent efforts of the Israeli government to de-Arabize and Judaize culture, and because of the process of urbanization. Educators, students, and oral historians distributed oral histories as pamphlets to promote cultural survival. Thus, oral history gave scholars the role of engaged intellectuals. Their work focused on refugees and rural ways of life, which were recurrent themes among artists, intellectuals, and publications of the Palestinian national movement.

Since 2000, oral history and ethnography shifted its focus to the experiences of young, urban, and working people. Young working women carved a niche for themselves in the oral history medium and in the discourse about sumud (steadfastness). In my work, the midwives were excellent users of oral history. They told long, sustained narratives of the self as struggling and working gendered persons who are independent financially and psychologically. They saw themselves as different from their mothers' generation, because they were the main breadwinners in their families, and different from the men of their own generation, because the men were either semi-employed or unemployed. The closure and job market were gendered in ways that made mobility difficult for many men to find employment. In this context, the men did not feel that oral history would depict their lives with dignity. On the other hand, the midwives in the oral histories presented a new and desirable type of classed femininity. A woman from a poor background with an education and a low-paid job who worked and struggled for decades could do well, be upwardly mobile, and live somewhat disengaged from male kin.

I learned that talk about birth and new beginnings brings out local stories about medical care. Thus, in a second part of the book, I explored the Palestinian medical infrastructure where the midwives worked and women gave birth. I first focused on the PLO's use and deployment of sumud funds, politics, and parallel institutionalization through the oral history of one of the main medical institutions in the Occupied Territories. It is about the way administrators and practitioners understood and remembered these politics. The chapter asks how men and women in the sumud institutions understand their work. Dr. Rami told the history of Maqassed Hospital as one closely connected to the sumud politics of the PLO. He described a centralized, top-down, high-tech hospital that ran big operations and was functional despite Israeli authorities' impediments and despite temporary losses of funding. It had the aura of a welfare state centralized institution.

The midwives at Makassed emphasized that the hospital was not the ideal entity it presented itself to be. All was not organized, rational, and smoothly productive. Sumud was a recurring theme among midwives, but it had acquired a new, social, and subaltern tonality, in addition to the nationalist slant taken for granted. They too felt that their steadfastness was directed toward the political predicament in which the occupation, in general, and the system of closures, in particular, had placed them. But they also felt that it was a matter of continuing to work in the face of conditions for which the Palestinian employer was also responsible. This form of sumud paralleled the combined national and social objectives of the 2000 intifada, as a whole, directed as it was against the occupation and against the Palestinian Authority, by whom they felt exploited. Furthermore, they explained how birth care at the most technologically advanced hospital was often given over the phone and that their family's lives were difficult because they had to work weeks on end in the dorms at the hospital and could not go home regularly.

I then turned to another type of health institution in Palestine: the mass-based participatory health movements that have become NGOs. I explored what participation looks like there and what it means to people. In the late 1970s, a group of doctors educated in the former Soviet Union started a health movement to resist Israeli occupation and break with the tradition of sumud institutions. They referred to themselves as ṣumūd-muqawim (resistant sumud) or the popular health movement. They constructed a movement that was different from the model of charitable associations where wealthy notables, businessmen, and states donate to institutions that redistribute to the needy. They saw their work as pushing people to demand healthcare as a right and to address class inequalities. The doctors themselves were part of a new class of leaders in Palestine. They were from rural backgrounds, although they lived in cities and were educated in the former Soviet Bloc. They started the movement by driving mobile clinics to the villages they were from and then started opening clinics in rural and underserved areas. The founding members of the movement tell the story of their beginnings, their personal awakenings, their work in resisting occupation, the mobile clinics, the institutionalization of the movement, the bureaucratization of the movement, and then the ways in which the movement turned into something similar to an NGO, dependent on foreign funding.

I then explored the site of the childbirth network that organized to assist births during the Second Intifada. Some of the founders of the popular health movement, who left it in the 1990s, were actively involved in the childbirth network. They were excited by the project and organized to get as many health workers as possible to collaborate with them. But some practitioners who assisted births in enclosed villages did not want to associate with the network. They found it already too institutionalized and preferred to work on a small, local level.

Finally, I circled back to new mothers' narratives about their births. Some had scathing critiques of the care they received. In certain cases, such as in the clinic of Dr. T, a newborn died at birth. The new mother and villagers circulated stories about the neonatal birth and the doctor's care. I heard stories in multiple forms, some in interviews and others as rumors or scandalous news. Often, the clinic or hospital would have to close down or fire a doctor because of the scandals. In some ways, these rumors and scandals are new mothers' and villagers' demands for better access to medical care.

It has been twenty years since I conducted my first fieldwork visit on birth. So many stories and experiences entangle themselves with fieldwork stories. Some stories and experiences changed things in me, as fieldwork did. I moved to Beirut, where I teach anthropology. I have given birth three times, and friends and family have also given birth. I discovered neighborhoods, villages, and institutions through my students' fieldwork in Lebanon. I did some fieldwork myself in Lebanon and listened to the narratives of mothers who had near-death experiences. I met doctors and health professionals in hospitals crushed by the inability to care for patients because of lack of funds in the government hospital in Beirut, as well as other doctors who fled their bombed out, underground, field hospital in Aleppo. In the middle of these events and throughout these years, I intermittently returned to Palestine to visit with my parents, friends, and interlocutors.

In the spring of 2018, my parents had to leave Palestine. After returning from travels, the Israeli authorities gave them a three-week visa, forbidding them to continue working in the Occupied Territories. Over the course of that month, at Birzeit University alone, where my father worked as a history professor and my mother as a researcher in public health and midwifery, nine other employees were barred from the Occupied Territories. They consulted lawyers and experts, but it was clear that they needed to leave. So, they packed their things, said goodbye to their friends, and left for Cyprus. Over the course of the thirty years that my parents lived in Palestine, the threat of being evicted or refused entry was always present. But their forced departure was nevertheless a shock, having to leave behind their lives.

I have not returned to Palestine since 2018. But it returns to me in whiffs of visions and voices. Sometimes I remember stones, trees, and words; sometimes I remember a common energy that would emerge regularly, at particular moments, to focus on a low-level struggle. Here, my field notes entry of October 24, 2003, describes one such moment, during the drive between Ramallah and Jerusalem:

I left Ramallah at 7:30 A.M. I got to Qalandia [main checkpoint on the road to Jerusalem] and decided to take a communal taxi through a back road ('ala allaffa, tariq anata). That was a mistake. I waited for the Ford minibus to fill with people before the driver started driving and we were surprised by a checkpoint at Jaba'. A checkpoint and a long string of cars. A long wait. An hour later, the taxi driver got to the soldiers at the checkpoint and it was our turn to be checked. Two soldiers peered into the van, first in the front seat then in the back. "Teudot, Teudot," [IDs in Hebrew] one of them said and made a movement with his head and eyes to signal that he wanted everyone's identity papers. When the driver noticed no one was moving to get their IDs, he started saying, "Give me your IDs. Give me your IDs." No one paid attention. Everyone pretended they had not heard anything for a few seconds that felt like hours. And one of the young men riding in the van said to the driver "are you providing them with your stupid services or what?" The soldier was still staring at the taxi riders one after the other. A few moments later, everyone started to look in their purses and pockets slowly, in slow motion. I had this image of a sort of slow down strike where workers adopt a go-slow tactic. The soldier went person by person. He would point to someone in the van and the person would in slow motion reach for his ID and in slow motion extend his hand to give the papers to the soldier. The soldier snatched one ID at a time. He was angry. And when he was done he yelled something in Hebrew to the driver. The driver did not respond. We waited and waited for the soldier to return with the driver's ID. He had just left us. An old woman asked the driver what the soldier had said, the driver answered that he had told him that when you speak to me you look at me and sit straight and you be alert. The old woman responded "samideen" [we are perseverant]. A half hour later, the soldier returned the driver's papers and made a hand gesture to him to go. Two kilometers later, another checkpoint. The old woman reiterated: "Oh god, keep us perseverant." The old woman invoked sumud to suggest to the driver to stay proud and continue his work. It had a calming effect in the minibus. I felt like the old woman rechanneled the mixture of anger, shame, and tension to a kind of low-level energy of patient struggle.

These memories mix themselves with what I have lived since my last visit. From these questions to diverse stories, I return to the site of displacement, catastrophe, loss, and the need to narrate. I contemplate the longue durée and human experience of these categories and reinterpret my corpus of storytelling as full of appearances of the living and of the people whose stories I do not hear.

References

Index

References

Abdel-Rahim, H., L. Wick, S. Halileh, S. Hassan Bitar, H. Chekir, G. Watt, and M. Khawaja. 2009. "Maternal and Child Health in the Occupied Palestinian Territory." *Lancet* 373, no. 9667: 967–77.

Abdo, Nahla. 2011. *Women in Israel: Race, Gender and Citizenship*. London: Zed Books.

Abou-Tabickh, Lilian. 2010. "Women's Masked Migration: Palestinian Women Explain Their Move Upon Marriage." In *Displaced at Home: Ethnicity and Gender among Palestinians in Israel*, edited by Rhoda Kanaaneh and Isis Nusair. Albany: State Univ. of New York Press.

———. 2012. "Migrants at Home: The Impact of Israeli Land Policy and Patrilocal Residence on Palestinian Women in Israel." In *Nationalism and Human Rights*, edited by G. Cheng. New York: Palgrave Macmillan.

Abu-Lughod, Lila. 1986. *Veiled Sentiments: Honor and Poetry in a Bedouin Society*. Berkeley: Univ. of California Press.

Aburish, Said K. 1998. *Arafat: From Defender to Dictator*. London: Bloomsbury.

Agamben, Giorgio. 1998. *Homo Sacer: Sovereign Power and Bare Life*. Stanford, CA: Stanford Univ. Press.

Ahmida, Ali. 1994. *The Making of Modern Libya: State Formation, Colonization, and Resistance. 1830-1932*. Albany: State Univ. of New York Press.

Al-Hardan, Anaheed. 2016. *Palestinians in Syria: Nakba Memories of Shattered Communities*. New York: Columbia Univ. Press.

Allan, Diana. 2007. "The Politics of Witness: Remembering and Forgetting 1948 in Shatila Camp." In *Nakba: Palestine, 1948 and the Claims of Memory*, edited by Ahmad Saadi and Lila Abu Lughod. New York: Columbia Univ. Press.

———. 2014. *Refugees of the Revolution: Experiences of Palestinian Exile*. Stanford, CA: Stanford Univ. Press.

Allen, Lori. 2008. "Getting by the Occupation: How Violence Became Normal during the Second Palestinian Intifada." *Cultural Anthropology* 23, no. 3: 453–87.

———. 2013. *The Rise and Fall of Human Rights: Cynicism and Politics in Occupied Palestine*. Stanford, CA: Stanford Univ. Press.

Al-Masri, Muzna. 2017. "Sensory Reverberations: Rethinking the Temporal and Experiential Boundaries of War Ethnography." *Contemporary Levant* 2, no. 1: 37–48.

Al-Usra, In'ash. 1973. *Dirasat fi l-mujtama' wa l-turath al-sha'bi al- Filastini: Qariat Termosa'iyya*. Beirut: Palestine Research Center.

Alvaro Alonso, Ruairí Brugha. 2006. "Rehabilitating the Health System after Conflict in East Timor: A Shift from NGO to Government Leadership." *Health Policy and Planning* 21, no. 3: 206–16.

Amiry, Suad. 2003. *Sharon and My Mother-in-Law: Ramallah Diaries*. New York: Anchor Books.

Anderson, Benedict. 1991. *Imagined Communities: Reflections on the Origin and Spread of Nationalism*. London: Verso.

Appadurai, Arjun. 2006. *Fear of Small Numbers*. Durham, NC: Duke Univ. Press.

Arendt, Hannah. 1958. *The Human Condition*. Chicago: Chicago Univ. Press.

Armstrong, Nancy. 1987. *Desire and Domestic Fiction: A Political History of the Novel*. Oxford: Oxford Univ. Press.

Bardenstein, Carol. 1997. "Raped Brides and Steadfast Others: Appropriations of Palestinian Motherhood." In *The Politics of Motherhood: Activist Voices from Left to Right*, edited by Jetter. Hanover, NH: Univ. Press of New England.

Barghouti, Mustafa. 2005. "Palestinian Defiance. Interview by Eric Hazan." *New Left Review* 32: 117–31.

Barghouti, Mustafa, and Rita Giacaman. 1990. "The Emergence of an Infrastructure of Resistance: The Case of Health." In *Intifada: Palestine at the Crossroads*, edited by Jamal Nassar and Roger Heacock, 73–90. New York: Praeger.

Bash, Ahmad Mustafa. 1998. *Tirat Haifa: karmeliyat al-judhur, filistiniyyat al-intima*. Damascus: Dar al-Shajara.

Blecher, Robert. 2002. "The Medicalization of Sovereignty: Medicine, Public Health, and Political Authority in Syria, 1861–1936." PhD diss., Stanford Univ.

Botmeh, Samia, and Gary Sotnik. 2007. *The Determinants of Female Labor Force Participation in the West Bank and Gaza Strip*. Jerusalem: Palestine Economic Policy Research Institute, MAS.

Boullata, Kamal. 2009. *Palestinian Art: from 1850 to the Present*. London: Saqi Books.

Caton, Steven. 1990. *Peaks of Yemen I Summon*. Berkeley: Univ. of California Press.

Choices and Challenges for Changing Childbirth Research Network. 2005. "Routines in Facility-Based Maternity Care: Evidence from the Arab World." *British Journal of Obstetrics and Gynecology* 112 (September): 1270–76.

Collier, Jane. 1986. "From Mary to Modern Woman: The Material Basis of Marianismo and Its Transformation in a Spanish Village." *American Ethnologist* 13, no. 1: 100–107.

Collins, John. 2004. *Occupied by Memory*. New York: New York Univ. Press.

cooke, miriam. 1987. *War's Other Voices: Women Writers on the Lebanese Civil War*. Syracuse: Syracuse Univ. Press.

Crapanzano, Vincent. 1980. *Tuhami: Portrait of a Moroccan*. Chicago: Univ. of Chicago Press.

Darwish, Mahmoud. 1993 [1964]. *Awraq al-Zaytun*. Beirut: Dar al-Awda.

———. 2013. *Memory for Forgetfulness*. Translated by Ibrahim Muhawi. Berkeley: Univ. of California Press.

Das, Veena. 1995. *Critical Events: An Anthropological Perspective on Contemporary India*. Delhi: Oxford Univ. Press.

Davis, Rochelle. 2011. *Palestinian Village Histories: Geographies of the Displaced*. Stanford, CA: Stanford Univ. Press.

Davis-Floyd, Robbie. 1992. *Birth as an American Rite of Passage*. Berkeley: Univ. of California Press.

Davis-Floyd, Robbie, and Carolyn Sargent. 1996. *Childbirth and Authoritative Knowledge: Cross-Cultural Knowledge*. Berkeley: Univ. of California Press.

Dewachi, Omar. 2017. *Ungovernable Life: Mandatory Medicine and Statecraft in Iraq*. Stanford, CA: Stanford Univ. Press.

Dick-Read, Grantly. 1933. *Natural Childbirth*. London: Heinemann Medical.

Doumani, Beshara. 2003. *Family History in the Middle East: Household, Property and Gender*. Albany: State Univ. of New York Press.

Dumit, Joseph. 2004. *Picturing Personhood: Pet Scans and Biomedical Identity*. Princeton, NJ: Princeton Univ. Press.

———. 2012. *Drugs for Life: How Pharmaceutical Companies Define Our Health*. Durham, NC: Duke Univ. Press.

Durkheim, Emile. 1951. *Suicide: A Study in Sociology*. New York: Free Press.

———. 2018. *The Elementary Forms of Religious Life*. Translated by Joseph Ward Swain. Minneola, NY: Dover Publications.

Fargues, Philippe. 2000. "Protracted National Conflict and Fertility Change: Palestinians and Israelis in the Twentieth Century." *Population and Development Review* 26, no. 3: 441–82.

Farsakh, Leila. 2005. *Palestinian Labor Migration to Israel: Labor, Land and Occupation.* London: Routledge.

Fassin, Didier. 2008. "The Humanitarian Politics of Testimony: Subjectification through Trauma in the Israeli-Palestinian Conflict." *Cultural Anthropology* 23, no. 3: 531–58.

Feldman, Ilana. 2015. "Looking for Humanitarian Purpose: Endurance and the Value of Lives in a Palestinian Refugee Camp." *Public Culture* 27, no. 3: 427–47.

———. 2018. *Life Lived in Relief: Humanitarian Predicaments and Palestinian Refugee Politics.* Berkeley: Univ. of California Press.

Fischer, Michael M.J. 1982. "Portrait of a Mullah: The Autobiography and Bildungsroman of Aqa Najafi-Quchani." *Persica* 10: 223–57.

———. 1983. "Ethnicity and the Postmodern Arts of Memory." In *Writing Culture: The Poetics and Politics of Ethnography,* edited by James Clifford and George Marcus. Berkeley: Univ. of California Press.

———. 2003. *Emergent Forms of Life and the Anthropological Voice.* Durham, NC: Duke Univ. Press.

Fleishman, Ellen. 2003. *The Nation and Its "New" Women: The Palestinian Women's Movement 1920–1948.* Berkeley: Univ. of California Press.

Foucault, Michel. 2004. *Naissance de la Biopolitique: Cours au Collège de France (1978–1979).* Paris: Gallimard.

Geertz, Hildred. 1978. "The Meaning of Family Ties." In *Meaning and Order in Moroccan Society,* edited by Clifford Geertz, Hildred Geertz, Laurence Rosen and Paul Hyman. Cambridge: Cambridge Univ. Press.

Giacaman, Rita, Yoke Rabaia, Viet Nguyen-Gillham, Rajaie Batniji, Raija-Leena Punamäki, and Derek Summerfield. 2011. "Mental Health, Social Distress and Political Oppression: The Case of the Occupied Palestinian Territory." *Global Public Health* 6, no. 5: 547–59.

Ginsburg, Faye, and Rayna Rapp, eds. 1995. *Conceiving the New World Order: The Global Politics of Reproduction.* Berkeley: Univ. of California Press.

Granqvist, Hilma. 1931. *Marriage Conditions in a Palestinian Village II.* Helsingfors, Sweden: Akademische Buchhandlung.

Guha, Ranajit, and Gayatri Chakravorty Spivak. 1988. *Selected Subaltern Studies.* Delhi: Oxford Univ. Press.

Hage, Ghassan. 1996. "Nationalist Anxiety or the Fear of Losing Your Other." *Australian Journal of Anthropology (TAJA),* August.

———. 2013. "Between Dependence and Independence: What Future for Palestine?" Keynote Presentation at Birzeit University Conference, Birzeit, West Bank.

Hage, Ghassan, ed. 2009. *Waiting*. Melbourne: Melbourne Univ. Press.

Hamdy, Sherine. 2012. *Our Bodies Belong to God: Organ Transplant, Islam and the Struggle for Human Dignity in Egypt*. Berkeley: Univ. of California Press.

Hamdy, Sherine, and Soha Bayoumi. 2016. "Egypt's Popular Uprising and the Stakes of Medical Neutrality." *Culture, Medicine and Psychiatry* 40, no. 2: 223–41.

Hammami, Rema. 2004. "On the Importance of Thugs: The Moral Economy of a Checkpoint." *Middle East Report* 231: 26–34.

———. 2010. "Qalandya: Jerusalem's Tora Bora and the Frontiers of Global Inequality." *Jerusalem Quarterly* 41: 29–51.

———. 1995. "NGOs: The Professionalization of Politics." *Race and Class* 37, no. 2: 51–63.

Hanafi, Sari, and Linda Tabar. 2005. *The Emergence of a Palestinian Globalized Elite: Donors, International Organizations and Local NGOs*. Jerusalem: Institute for Jerusalem Studies and Muwatin.

Harlow, Barbara. 1996. *After Lives: Legacies of Revolutionary Writing*. London: Verso.

Hasso, Frances. 2005. *Repression and Gender Politics in Occupied Palestine and Jordan*. Syracuse, NY: Syracuse Univ. Press.

Heacock, Roger. 2018. "Seizing Time and Space: The Intifada, Adel Yahya, Palestine, and the World." In *Reclaiming the Past for the Future: Oral History, Craft, and Archaeology*, edited by Reinhard Bernbek et al., 221–40. Berlin: ex oriente e.V.

Heacock, Roger, and Alaa Jradat, eds. 2020. *The 1987 Intifada: A People's Transformation*. Beirut: Institute for Palestine Studies.

Heacock, Roger, and Jamal Nassar, eds. 1990. *Intifada: Palestine at the Crossroads*. New York: Praeger.

Hermez, Sami. 2017. *War Is Coming: Between Past and Future Violence in Lebanon*. Philadelphia: Univ. of Pennsylvania Press.

Hilterman, Joost. 1991. *Behind the Intifada: Labor and Women's Movements in the Occupied Territories*. Princeton, NJ: Princeton Univ. Press.

Hogan, Margaret, Kyle J. Foreman, Mohsen Naghavi, Stephanie Y. Ahn, Mengru Wang, Susanna M. Makela, Alan D. Lopez, Rafael Lozano, and Christopher J.L. Murray. 2010. "Maternal Mortality for 181 Countries, 1980–2008:

A Systematic Analysis of Progress towards Millennium Development Goal." *Lancet* 375, no. 9726: 1609–23.

Office of the High Commissioner for Human Rights (OHCHR). 2005. *Issue of Palestinian Pregnant Women Giving Birth at Israeli Checkpoints.* A/60/324. https://www.un.org/unispal/document/auto-insert-183639/.

Jabra, Ibrahim Jabra. 1995. *The First Well: A Bethlehem Boyhood.* Translated by Issa Boullata. Fayetteville: Univ. of Arkansas Press.

Jackson, Michael. 2002. *The Politics of Storytelling: Violence, Transgression and Intersubjectivity.* Copenhagen: Museum Tusculanum Press.

Jad, Islah. 1990. "From Salons to Popular Committees: Palestinian Women, 1919–1989." In *Intifada: Palestine at a Crossroads*, edited by Roger Heacock and Issam Nassar. New York: Praeger.

———. 2018. *Palestinian Women's Activism: Nationalism, Secularism, Islamism.* Syracuse, NY: Syracuse Univ. Press.

Jamal, Amal. 2016. "Conflict Theory, Temporality and Transformative Temporariness: Lessons from Israel Palestine." *Constellations: An International Journal of Critical and Democratic Theory* 23, no. 3: 365–77.

James, Erica. 2004. "The Political Economy of 'Trauma' in Haiti in the Democratic Era of Insecurity." *Culture, Medicine and Psychiatry* 28, no. 2: 127–49.

Jubeh, Nazmi. 2021. "Hay al-Shaykh Jarrah wa-maarakat al-baqa.'" *Journal of Palestine Studies* 127: 34–66.

Johnson, Penny. 2006. "Living Together in a Nation in Fragments." In *Living Palestine: Family, Survival and Mobility in Palestine*, edited by Lisa Taraki. Syracuse, NY: Syracuse Univ. Press.

Joseph, Suad. 1994. "Brother/Sister Relationships: Connectivity, Love, and Power in the Reproduction of Patriarchy in Lebanon." *American Ethnologist* 21, no. 1: 50–73.

———. 1999. "Introduction." In *Intimate Selving in Arab Families*, edited by Suad Joseph, 1–17. Syracuse, NY: Syracuse Univ. Press.

———. 2010. *Rethinking Arab Family Projects.* Arab Families Working Group.

———. 2018. *Arab Family Studies: Critical Reviews.* Syracuse, NY: Syracuse Univ. Press.

Kanaaneh, Rhoda. 2002. *Birthing the Nation: Strategies of Palestinian Women in Israel.* Berkeley: Univ. of California Press.

Kanafani, Ghassan. 1969. *A'id Ila Haifa (Return to Haifa).* In *Al-Athar al-Kamila (Collected Works).* Vol. 1. Beirut: Dar al-Tali'a.

Kandiyoti, Deniz. 1988. "Bargaining with Patriarchy." *Gender and Society* 2, no. 3: 274–90.

Katz, Jonathan Ned. 1990. "The Invention of Heterosexuality." *Socialist Review* 20 (January–March): 7–34.

Khalidi, Rashid. 1997. *Palestinian Identity*. New York: Columbia Univ. Press.

Khalidi, Walid. 1991. *Before Their Diaspora: A Photographic History of the Palestinians 1876-1948*. Washington, DC: Institute for Palestine Studies.

Khalili, Laleh. 2004. "Grassroot Commemorations: Remembering the Land in the Camps of Lebanon." *Journal of Palestine Studies* 34, no. 1: 6–22.

Khayyat, Munira. 2020. "On Living through Plagues and Wars in Lebanon." *Anthropology News Website*. https://www.anthropology-news.org/articles/on-living-through-plagues-and-wars-in-lebanon/.

Khuri, Fuad. 1975. *From Village to Suburb: Order and Change in Greater Beirut*. Chicago: Univ. of Chicago Press.

Di Leonardo, Michaela. 1987. "The Female World of Cards and Holidays: Women, Families, and the Work of Kinship." *Signs* 12: 440–53.

Lévi-Strauss, Claude. 1961. *Tristes Tropiques*. Translated by John Russel. New York: Criterion Books.

Lockman, Zachary, and Joel Beinin, eds. 1989. *Intifada: The Palestinian Uprising against Israeli Occupation*. Boston: South End Press.

MacIntyre, Alasdair. 1981. *After Virtue: A Study in Moral Theory*. Notre Dame, IN: Univ. of Notre Dame Press.

Maffi, Irene. 2013. *Women, Health and the State in the Middle East: The Politics and Culture of Childbirth in Jordan*. New York: I.B. Tauris.

Malki, Majdi. 2005. "Surmonter l'Intifada d'Al-Aqsa: Entraide Sociale et Clientelisme en Palestine." *Etudes Rurales* (January): 201–17.

Malki, Majdi and Hassan Ladadwa. 2018. *Tahawulat al-mujtama' al-falastini mundhu sanat 1948: jadaliyyat al-fuqdan wa-tahadiyyat al-baqa'*. Beirut: Institute for Palestine Studies.

Manaa, Adel. 2016. *Nakba wa-Baqa': Hikayat falastiniyyin zhallu fi Haifa wa-l-Jalil*. Beirut: Institute for Palestine Studies.

Martin, Emily. 1987. *The Woman in the Body: A Cultural Analysis of Reproduction*. Boston: Beacon Press.

———. 1994. *Flexible Bodies: The Role of Immunity in American Culture from the Age of Polio to the Age of AIDS*. Boston: Beacon Press.

Massad, Joseph. 2007. *Desiring Arabs*. Chicago: Univ. of Chicago Press.

Mataria, Awad, Rana Khatib, Cam Donaldson, Thomas Bossert, David J. Hunter, Fahed Alsayed, and Jean-Paul Moatti. 2009. "Health in the Occupied Palestinian Territory: The Health-Care System: An Assessment and Reform Agenda." *Lancet* 373, no. 9670: 1207–17.

Mattingly, Cheryl. 1998. *Healing Dramas and Clinical Plots: The Narrative Structure of Experience*. Cambridge: Cambridge Univ. Press.

Mauss, Marcel. 1990. *The Gift: The Form and Reason for Exchange in Archaic Societies*. Translated by W. D. Halls. New York: W. W. Norton.

Meari, Lena. 2014a. "Reconsidering Trauma: Towards a Palestinian Community Psychology." *Journal of Community Psychology* 43, no. 1: 76–86.

———. 2014b. "Sumud, A Palestinian Theory of Confrontation in Colonial Prisons." *South Atlantic Quarterly* 113, no. 3: 2014.

Meeker, Michael. 1979. *Literature and Violence in North Arabia*. Cambridge: Cambridge Univ. Press.

Mitchell, Laura. 2010. "Coping, Closure and Gendered Life Transitions: Palestinians' Responses to the Erosion of Male Breadwinning Work." *FAFO Report*. https://www.fafo.no/zoo-publikasjoner/fafo-rapporter/coping-closure-and-gendered-life-transitions.

Moghnieh, Lamia. 2021. "Infrastructure of Suffering: Trauma, Sumud and the Politics of Violence and Aid in Lebanon." *Medicine, Anthropology, Theory* 8, no. 1: 1–26.

Muhawi, Ibrahim, and Sharif Kanaana. 1989. *Speak Bird, Speak Again: Palestinian Arab Folk Tales*. Berkeley: Univ. of California Press.

Nashef, Ismail. 2008. *Palestinian Political Prisoners: Identity and Community*. New York: Routledge.

Nazzal, Nafez. 1978. *The Palestinian Exodus from Galilee: 1948*. Beirut: Institute for Palestine Studies.

Nimr, Sonia. 1990. "The Arab Revolt in Palestine: A Study Based on Oral Sources." PhD diss., Univ. of Exeter.

Obeid, Michelle. 2019. *Border Lives: An Ethnography of a Lebanese Town in Changing Times*. Boston: Brill.

Oliveira, Gabrielle. 2018. *Motherhood Across Borders: Immigrants and Their Children in Mexico and New York*. New York: New York Univ. Press.

Perdigon, Sylvain. 2008. "La Corniche des Célibataires : l'intimité à l'épreuve du transnationalisme chez les jeunes de Jal al-Baher, Liban-Sud." In *Les Métamorphoses du Mariage au Moyen Orient*, edited by Barbara Drieskens, 33–46. Presse de l'IFPO. https://books.openedition.org/ifpo/450?lang=en.

———. 2018. "Life on the Cusp of Form: In Search of Worldliness with Palestinian Refugees in Tyre, Lebanon." *Hau: Journal of Ethnographic Theory* 8, no. 3: 566–83.

Perrenas, R.S. 2001. "Mothering from a Distance: Emotions, Gender and Intergenerational Relations in Filipino Transnational Families." *Feminist Studies* 27, no. 2: 261–90.

Peteet, Julie. 1991. *Gender in Crisis: Women and the Palestinian Resistance Movement.* New York: Columbia Univ. Press.

———. 2017. *Space and Mobility in Palestine.* Bloomington: Indiana Univ. Press.

———. 2018. "Closure's Temporality: The Cultural Politics of Time and Waiting." *South Atlantic Quarterly* 117, no. 1: 43–64.

Pinto, Sarah. 2008. *Where There Is No Midwife: Birth and Loss in Rural India.* New York: Bergahn Books.

Povinelli, Elizabeth. 2006. *The Empire of Love: Toward a Theory of Intimacy, Genealogy and Carnality.* Durham, NC: Duke Univ. Press.

Powell, Libby. 2011. "Palestinian Newborns Are Dying at Checkpoints." *New Internationalist*, July. https://newint.org/blog/2011/07/13/palestine-birth-at-checkpoint.

Radin, Paul. 1999 [1926]. *Crashing Thunder: The Autobiography of an American Indian.* Ann Arbor: Univ. of Michigan Press.

Renan, Ernest. 1998. *Qu'est-ce qu'une Nation?* Paris: Editions Mille et une Nuits.

Richter-Devroe, Sophie. 2018. *Women's Political Activism in Palestine: Peace-Building, Resistance, Survival.* Champaign, IL: Univ. of Illinois Press.

Saadi, Ahmad. 2002. "Catastrophe, Memory and Identity: Al-Nakbah as a Component of Palestinian Identity." *Israel Studies* 7, no. 2 (Summer): 175–98.

Saadi, Ahmad, and Lila Abu-Lughod, eds. 2007. *1948 and the Claims of Memory.* New York: Columbia Univ. Press.

Sadler, Michelle et al. 2016. "Moving beyond Disrespect and Abuse: Addressing the Structural Dimensions of Obstetric Violence." *Reproductive Health Matters* 24, no. 27: 47–55.

Said, Edward. 1999. *After the Last Sky: Palestinian Lives.* New York: Columbia Univ. Press.

Sakakini, Khalil. 2003. *The Memoirs of Khalil Sakakini.* Edited by Faisal Darraj. Ramallah: Khalil Sakakini Cultural Center.

Salam-Khalidi, Anbara. 2013. *Memoirs of an Early Arab Feminist: The Life and Activism of Anbara Salam Khalidi.* Translated by Tarif Khalidi. London: Pluto Press.

Saleh, Elizabeth. 2016. "The Master Cockroach: Scrap Metal and Syrian Labor in Beirut's Informal Economy." *Contemporary Levant* 1, no. 2: 93–107.

———. 2017. "A Tangled Web of Lies: Reflections on Ethnographic Fieldwork with Turkmen Women on the Side of the Road in Beirut." *Contemporary Levant* 2, no. 1: 55–60.

Saleh, Elizabeth, and Adrian Zakar. 2018. "The Joke Is on Us: Irony and Community in a Beirut Scrapyard." *Anthropology Today* 34, no. 3: 3–6.

Salih, Ruba. 2018. "Refugees and Cathartic Politics: From Human Rights to the Right to Be Human." *South Atlantic Quarterly* 117, no. 1: 135–55.

Sanal, Aslihan. 2011. *New Organs Within Us: Transplants and the Moral Economy*. Durham, NC: Duke Univ. Press.

Sanbar, Elias. 2001. "Out of Place, Out of Time." *Mediterranean Historical Review* 16: 87–94.

Sandler, Shmuel, and Hillel Frisch. 1984. *Israel, the Palestinians, and the West Bank*. Lexington, Massachusetts: Lexington Books.

Sayigh, Rosemary. 1979. *Palestinians: From Peasants to Revolutionaries*. London: Zed Books.

———. 1998. "Palestinian Camp Women as Tellers of History." *Journal of Palestine Studies* 27, no. 2: 42–58.

———. 2002. "The History of Palestinian Oral History: Individual Vitality and Institutional Paralysis." *Al-Jana* 2: 64–66.

Sayigh, Yezid. 1997. *Armed Struggle and the Search for State: The Palestinian National Movement 1949–1993*. Oxford: Clarendon Press.

Scheid, Kirsten. 2013. "Between the Promise of Life and Its Fragility: The Arab Body in the Khalid Shoman Collection." In *Arab Art Histories: The Khalid Shoman Collection*. Amman, Jordan: Khalid Shoman Foundation.

Schiff, Ze'ev, and Ehud Ya'ari. 1990. *Intifada: The Palestinian Uprising—Israel's Third Front*. New York: Simon & Schuster.

Segal, Lotte Buch. 2016. *No Place for Grief: Martyrs, Prisoners, and Mourning in Contemporary Palestine*. Philadelphia: Univ. of Pennsylvania Press.

Shalhoub-Kevorkian, Nadera. 2012. *Birthing in Occupied East Jerusalem: Palestinian Women's Experiences of Pregnancy and Delivery*. Jerusalem: YWCA.

Shehadeh, Raja. 1982. *The Third Way. A Journal of Life in the West Bank*. London: Quartet Books.

Shoaibi, Hala. 2011. "Childbirth at Checkpoints in the Occupied Palestinian Territory." *Lancet Abstracts*, July. https://www.thelancet.com/pb/assets/raw/Lancet/abstracts/palestine/palestine2011-4.pdf.

Sholkamy, Hania. 2003. "Rationales for Kin Marriages in Rural Upper Egypt." In *The New Arab Family*, edited by Nicholas Hopkins, 62–79. Cairo: American Univ. of Cairo Press.

Shostak, Marjorie. 1981. *Nisa: The Life and Words of a Kung Woman*. Cambridge, MA: Harvard Univ. Press.

Shreef, Abu and Bassam. 2005. *Yasser Arafat*. Beirut: Riyad El Rayyes

Slyomovics, Susan. 1998. *The Object of Memory: Arab and Jew Narrate the Palestinian Village*. Philadelphia: Univ. of Pennsylvania Press.

Spivak, Gayatri Chakravorty. 1988. "Deconstructing Historiography". In *The Selected Subaltern Studies*, edited by Ranajit Guha and Gayatri Chakravorty Spivak, 3–35. Oxford: Oxford Univ. Press.

Stringer, Heather. 2018. "Psychologists Respond to a Mental Health Crisis at the Border." *American Psychological Association News*. https://www.apa.org/news/apa/2018/border-family-separation.

Swedenburg, Ted. 1990. "The Palestinian Peasant as National Signifier." *Anthropological Quarterly* 63: 18–30.

Tamari, Salim, and Issam Nassar, eds. 2003. *Ottoman Jerusalem in the Jawharieh Memoirs: The First Book of the Musician Wassef Jawharieh 1904–1917*. Beirut: Institute for Palestine Studies.

Taraki, Lisa. 1990. "The Development of Political Consciousness among Palestinians of the Occupied Territories." In *Intifada: Palestine at the Crossroads*. New York: Praeger.

———. 2003. *Memories of a Revolt: The 1936–1939 Rebellion and the Palestinian National Past*. Fayetteville: Univ. of Arkansas Press.

———. 2013. "Man sana'a Ramallah?" Presented at the conference titled "Stratajiyyat al-tawafuq wa-l-baqa' 'ind al-falastiniyyin fi l-watan." In'ash al-Usra Society, Ramallah. https://www.youtube.com/watch?v=4ciaxJ3AI-s.

Tawil-Souri, Helga. 2009. "New Palestinian Centers: An Ethnography of the Checkpoint Economy." *International Journal of Cultural Studies* 12: 217–35.

———. 2011. "Colored Identity: The Politics and Materiality of ID Cards in Palestine/Israel." *Social Text* 29, no. 2 (Summer): 67–97.

———. 2012. "Uneven Borders, Coloured (Im)Mobilities: ID Cards in Palestine-Israel." *Geopolitics* 17: 153–76.

Taylor, Verta. 1996. *Rock-a-by Baby: Feminism, Self-Help, and Postpartum Depression*. New York: Routledge.

Tekce, Belgin. 2004. "Paths of Marriage in Istanbul: Arranging Choices and Choice of Arrangements." *Ethnography* 5, no. 2: 173–201.

Toukan, Hanan. 2021. *The Politics of Art: Dissent and Cultural Diplomacy in Lebanon, Palestine and Jordan*. Stanford, CA: Stanford Univ. Press.

Tuqan, Fadwa. 1990. *A Mountainous Journey: An Autobiography*. Translated by Olive Kenny. London: Women's Press.

Vansina, Jan. 1985. Oral Tradition as History. Madison: Univ. of Wisconsin Press.

Welchman, Lynn. 2000. *Beyond the Code: Muslim Family Law and the Sharia Judiciary in the Palestinian West Bank*. The Hague: Kluwer Law International.

White, Hayden. 1973. *Metahistory: The Historical Imagination in Nineteenth-Centry Europe*. Baltimore: Johns Hopkins Univ. Press.

Wick, Livia. 2008. "Building the Infrastructure, Modeling the Nation: The Case of Birth in Palestine." *Culture, Medicine and Psychiatry* 32: 328–57.

———. 2011. "The Practice of Waiting Under Closure in Palestine." *City and Society* 23 (September): 24–44.

Williams, C.R. 2018. "Obstetric Violence: A Latin American Legal Response to Mistreatment during Childbirth." *An International Journal of Obstetrics and Gynaecology* 24, no. 47: 47–55.

Yahya, Adel. 1990a. "Oral History: Methodological and Practical Issues." In *Afaq Filistiniyya*. Birzeit: Birzeit Univ.

———. 1990b. "The Role of the Refugee Camps." In *Intifada: Palestine and the Crossroads*, edited by Jamal Nassar and Roger Heacock, 91–106. New York: Praeger.

———. 1999a. "Introduction." *In PACE Tour Guide of the West Bank and Gaza Strip, Palestine: Historical and Archaeological Guide*. Ramallah: Al-mu'assasa al-falastiniyya li-l-tabadul al-thaqafi (PACE).

———. 1999b. *The Palestinian Refugees, 1948–1998: An Oral History*. Ramallah: Al-mu'assasa al-falastiniyya li-l-tabadul al-thaqafi (PACE).

———. 2002. *Bayna intifadatayn: Al-Tarikh al-shafawi—Dalil al-bahithin wa-l-mu'allimin wa-l-talaba*. Ramallah: Al-mu'assasa al-falastiniyya li-l-tabadul al-thaqafi (PACE).

———. 2006. *Qissat Mukhayam: Al-Jalazun – Tarikh Shafawi*. Ramallah: Al-mu'assasa al-falastiniyya li-l-tabadul al-thaqafi (PACE).

Yahya, Adel, Mahmud Ibrahim, and Thomas Ricks. 1994. *Man Yasna' al-Tarikh? Al-Tajriba al-Filastiniya fi l-tarikh al-shafawi – Dalil al-bahithin wa-l-mu'allimin wa-l-talaba*. Ramallah: Tamer Institute for Community Education.

Zamir, Israel. 1979. "The Market of Children at Erez Junction." *MERIP Reports* 74: 23–24.

Index

institutions and, 105; novels and
middle, 92; peasants, 54, 56, 75, 78–79,
81–83, 81n3, 116; working, 7, 8, 22
closure (*al-taskīr*): birth numbers under,
120–21; birth stories under, xv–xix,
20, 23, 115–16, 137–48; with colonial
settlement policies, 36–37; families
separated by, xiv, xix, 21, 24–25,
30, 32, 33, 40, 71, 100, 115, 151; life
shrinking and interrupted by, xiv, 29,
33, 116–17; mobile clinics and, 130;
policy restrictions, xiii–xiv, 35–36,
100; sumud and, 113–15; wage labor
and, 87
Collier, Jane, 31n8
colonialism, 37, 55, 76, 77, 110
colonial settlement policies, 36–37
Communist Party, 133, 136
communities, 80, 145; mobile clinics, 14,
127, 128–37, 148, 156; oral histories
and language from older generation
of, 50–51, 70–71
connective selves, 93–94
cooke, miriam, 7
Crapanzano, Vincent, 48
critical event, 4
Cuba, 77
culture. *See* rural culture
curfews (*man'al-tajawwul*): announcing,
xiii; cooperation and life under, 145;
on Ramallah, 138–39; television with,
xiv–xv. *See also* closure
"curse of sumud" (*la'nat assumūd*), 85n5
custody. *See* child custody

Dar al-Shajara publishers, 80
Darwish, Mahmoud, 56
Das, Veena, 4
daughters, mothers and, 30, 31, 40, 43, 45

Davis-Floyd, Robbie, 34
deaths: birth and, 129, 137, 138, 147, 156;
checkpoints with labor and, 20n1;
ethnic cleansing, 7, 8, 76; massacres,
14n4, 60, 127
Declaration of Principles (1993), 112n10
Democratic Front for the Liberation of
Palestine (DFLP), 77, 77n1
demonstrations, checkpoints, 59
depression: exhaustion and, 63; postpartum, 30
Destroyed Palestinian Villages series, 79
DFLP (Democratic Front for the Liberation of Palestine), 77, 77n1
Dheishe refugee camp, 129–30
Dirbass, Sahera, 80
discipline, 106
dispossession, 8, 38, 81
Divine Intervention (film), 35n12
divorce, child custody and, 27–28, 32,
61–65, 90, 125
doctors, 29, 59, 157; birth stories and,
xv–xviii, 23, 24, 144–46; cell phone
numbers of, xvin3; class divisions
and, 132; closure and, 115–16, 146;
communities and, 134; educated in
Soviet Union, 14, 26, 127, 155–56; at
Makassed Hospital, 117–18, 121–22,
128–29; medical malpractice and, 13,
15; midwives and, 123n20, 138n6;
number of, 137; oral histories and, 9,
88n6; popular health movement and,
14–15, 127–48, 155; with psychological care, 135; in refugee camps,
129–30; social services funding
coopting, 104; sovereignty and, 106;
in sumud institutions, 99; vilification of, 13; women, 122n18, 128–29,
134–35, 139–41, 145–46; with women
birthing, xv–xviii, 3, 11–12

Livia Wick is an associate professor of anthropology at the American University of Beirut.

Printed in the USA
CPSIA information can be obtained
at www.ICGtesting.com
CBHW031238230324
5612CB00002B/9

9 780815 637882